"Reading this devotional feels like you're chatting with your best girlfriends over lunch! These women make you feel like they know you—that they know what it feels like to be you. I love the variety and short length of each daily entry—you can read one in the time it takes to finish your morning coffee! Practical, sweet, and inspiring, *Trusting God* will help you do just that. And by the last page, you too will have some new girlfriends—Mary, Gwen, and Sharon!"

—JENNIFER ROTHSCHILD, author of *Self Talk, Soul Talk*
and *Lessons I Learned in the Dark*

"Girlfriends in God—Gwen, Sharon, and Mary—are some of the wisest women I know. My friends make trusting God seem simple, possible, and attainable. A girlfriend is someone who watches out for you, encourages you, and provides opportunity for you—and that is exactly what you will experience from these Girlfriends in God. If your life is feeling unstable, unsure, unreliable, or the path feels unknown, *Trusting God* will keep you under God's umbrella of tender-loving care."

—PAM FARREL, relationship specialist, international speaker,
author of best-selling *Men Are Like Waffles, Women Are Like
Spaghetti* and *The 10 Best Decisions a Woman Can Make*

"Trusting God in this world of uncertainty and economic upheaval isn't easy. We all need to learn, relearn, or be reminded daily of the truth that God can be trusted for each day's problems. True to their real and relatable style, this wonderful Girlfriends in God devotional is just what you need to encourage your heart and refresh your spirit."

—GEORGIA SHAFFER, licensed psychologist in Pennsylvania
and author of *Taking Out Your Emotional Trash*

TRUSTING GOD

A *Girlfriends*
IN GOD
FAITH ADVENTURE

TRUSTING GOD

Sharon Jaynes
Gwen Smith
Mary Southerland

MULTNOMAH
BOOKS

TRUSTING GOD
PUBLISHED BY MULTNOMAH BOOKS
12265 Oracle Boulevard, Suite 200
Colorado Springs, Colorado 80921

ISBN 978-1-60142-393-1
ISBN 978-1-60142-394-8 (electronic)

Published in the United States by WaterBrook Multnomah, an imprint of the Crown Publishing Group, a division of Random House Inc., New York.

MULTNOMAH and its mountain colophon are registered trademarks of Random House Inc.

Library of Congress Cataloging-in-Publication Data
Jaynes, Sharon.
    Trusting God : a girlfriends in God devotional / Sharon Jaynes, Gwen Smith, Mary Southerland. — 1st ed.
        p. cm.
    ISBN 978-1-60142-393-1 — ISBN 978-1-60142-394-8 (electronic)
    1. Christian women—Prayers and devotions. 2. Trust in God—Christianity—Prayers and devotions. I. Smith, Gwen, 1970– II. Southerland, Mary. III. Title.
    BV4844.J39 2011
    242'.643—dc23

                                    2011028972

Printed in the United States of America
2011—First Edition

10 9 8 7 6 5 4 3 2 1

Thank God for girlfriends!
This book is dedicated to our many Girlfriends in God
all around the world. We look forward to the day we see
your faces and hear your voices as we sing praises to our
God and King for all eternity. Until then, we're so
thankful that God has allowed us to do life together.
1 Thessalonians 2:8

Contents

Girlfriends Talk About Trusting God

T*rust.* Now that's a tough word to wrap your heart around. On the one hand, you celebrate and cherish those people with whom you can safely share anything and everything—your hopes and dreams, your faults and failures, the good times and the bad. No doubt about it—a friend you can fully trust is a priceless treasure.

On the other hand, how many times have you heard the phrase, "Just trust me," only to be disappointed or disillusioned? How many times have you put your faith in and counted on a person to do the right thing only to be deflated and discouraged? How many times have those words "Just trust me" turned out to be nothing more than an empty promise or a primer for disaster? Is anyone trustworthy these days?

What is trust? Webster's dictionary defines it this way: "To have faith or trust in, to rely on (someone) to do something or permit someone to use something in the proper way, to believe, to confide (someone or something) to a person's responsible care, to commit someone or something to the responsible care of (a person), to have faith in God."

Your life may be blessed with people you can trust—friends who really do have your best interests at heart and are there when you need them. Your life may also be littered with people you've trusted who have let you down. Perhaps you've got scars to remind you of people who've held your heart carelessly, walked away flippantly, or broken their word unapologetically. It has happened to all of us. And the hurt from a broken trust can make it difficult to count on people again.

But here's some good news: God is not human. God never changes. He is the same yesterday, today, and tomorrow. He will never leave us or forsake us. He says what He means and means what He says. God cares for you unceasingly, provides for you immeasurably, and loves you unconditionally. And you really can trust Him.

As Girlfriends in God (GiG), we are learning to trust God as we walk through good times and as we celebrate life-wins. We are also learning to trust God through trials and struggles like the ones you may be facing. The storms may be a bit different in nature, but they are storms nonetheless. We want to share our lives with you, and we hope the truths we've learned will help you deepen your trust in God.

Our Girlfriends in God theme verse is found in 1 Thessalonians 2:8: "We loved you so much, we were delighted to share with you not only the gospel of God but *our lives* as well." So in these pages we have opened our hearts and homes and invited you to take a peek inside. But that invitation comes with a warning—our lives are sometimes quite messy.

The apostle Paul instructed all Christians to "put on the full armor of God." It's a pretty snazzy outfit: the helmet of salvation, the breastplate of righteousness, the belt of truth, the sword of the Spirit, the sandals of the gospel of peace, and the shield of faith (Ephesians 6:13–17). A woman dressed in that power suit is armed and danger-

ous when the Enemy comes snooping around. While these verses tell of a figurative or spiritual armor, the actual armor soldiers wore during the time of Paul was fascinating—especially the shield. Shields were often made of heavy leather, which soldiers soaked in water to help extinguish the fiery darts the enemy shot at them. And the shields—oh, we're so excited to tell you this—the shields had hooks on the sides. Why? We thought you'd never ask. The shields had hooks on the sides so that, in difficult situations, the soldiers could link their shields together and march into battle as one.

Girlfriend, that is exactly what we want to do with you in the pages of this book. We want to hook shields with you and march as one. We want to lock arms with you, connect our hearts with yours, and learn how to seek and trust God together.

No matter how you choose to work through this book—on your own, with a prayer partner, with a group of friends, or with a GiG group—we are with you. At the end of each week, you'll find questions to ponder. We've called it "Now It's Your Turn," and that's exactly what it is—your turn. We've taken you on our holy field trips, and then it's your turn to tell about yours. We'd love to hear from you. We've set up a special page on our website so you can share what you've learned about trusting God. Just log onto www.Girl friendsInGod.com and click on the "Trusting God" page to tell us your story.

Now, let's get started on our journey to trusting God!

Girlfriends
IN GOD

Sharon Jaynes, Gwen Smith, and Mary Southerland

Bailing on God

Mary Southerland

Today's Truth
Trust God from the bottom of your heart. (Proverbs 3:5, MSG)

Friend to Friend
I absolutely love being a grandmother and wholeheartedly agree with the familiar adage, "If I had known grandchildren were so wonderful, I would have had them first!" Our fifteen-month-old granddaughter, Lelia Kay, sparkles with joy and has an infectious laugh that instantly captures your heart and compels you to laugh along with her. Consequently, our son, Jered, is always looking for ways to make her laugh. On a recent visit, he proudly demonstrated one of the new "tricks" he had taught Lelia. I was horrified!

Jered came home from work, scooped up his squealing daughter in his arms and grabbed her in a big hug. Lelia wrapped her little arms around her daddy's neck and then firmly planted a noisy kiss on his cheek. Tears filled my eyes when I heard Jered whisper, "I love you, Lelia." It was definitely a Kodak moment that left me totally unprepared for the moment that followed.

Lelia giggled, grabbed her daddy's shirt with both hands and

looked up at Jered, a mischievous sparkle in her eyes. I instantly recognized that sparkle and mentally added it to the list of things she had inherited from her daddy. Jered looked over at me and said, "Watch, Mom!" He tightened his hold on his daughter's chubby little legs and said, "Bail, Lelia!"

Surely, I had heard him wrong. Nope! My precious grandbaby immediately fell backward through the air, arms and hands dangling loosely over her head, swinging her little body through her daddy's firmly planted legs, laughing hysterically. My stomach fell and my mouth flew open as I watched her repeat this terrifying toddler version of bungee jumping. Not once did Lelia seem to be afraid. As far as I could tell, there was not the slightest hesitation on her part. I did not see an ounce of caution as she totally abandoned herself to the security of her father's arms—creating a beautiful and profound illustration of childlike faith.

That picture of faith took on a whole new meaning as we replayed it over dinner. "I have to be careful," Jered said. "Lelia will sometimes bail on me when I'm not expecting it." (Yes, that statement did increase my prayer life.) I looked at my son and, as I had so many times over the years, marveled at his strength, thinking of the countless hours he has spent lifting weights, playing football, and now building and remodeling homes. Jered's massive arms and shoulders are a testimony to his discipline and power. No wonder Lelia feels safe and secure in those arms.

I decided then and there that I want to be like Lelia. I want my faith in God to grow to the place where I can bail on God and totally abandon myself to my Father's safe, strong arms, secure in the knowledge that He will catch me when I fall. I want to obey God without fear, trusting Him to be all I need. I want to depend on and experience God's power and strength as I plunge into His plan for my life,

knowing that He is aware of every step I take, that He monitors every breath I breathe and sees every tear I cry.

It can be scary to trust God if we insist on fully understanding the step of faith He is asking us to take. Proverbs 3:5 assures us that we really can trust God from the bottom of our hearts—with every part of our lives. We tend to focus on what we can see and explain instead of choosing to focus on God and His promises. We need to grow and mature in Christ, but we also need to remain childlike in our faith.

Jered has never dropped Lelia. It probably has not even occurred to her that her father could or would drop her. Lelia's trust in her daddy is complete and whole. And I can assure you that Jered delights in that trust and will do everything he can to protect it. God is like that too. He celebrates even our tiniest step of faith and rejoices when we abandon ourselves to Him. How about you? Are you ready to bail into the arms of God?

Let's Pray

Father, I thank You for the strength and power of Your love. I praise You for Your faithfulness in my life. I long to believe You wholly, and I want to walk in a radical obedience to Your truth. Help me to choose faith over fear and trust over doubt. Teach me to rest in Your arms and trust Your heart, even when I don't understand Your process. I choose to place my faith in You. In Jesus's name, amen.

He's Got the Whole World in His Hands

Sharon Jaynes

Today's Truth

For he will command his angels concerning you to guard you in all your ways. (Psalm 91:11)

Friend to Friend

It was a beautiful crisp February morning when Steve and I traveled from our college town of Chapel Hill, North Carolina, to Charlotte to announce our engagement to Steve's family. The night before, God had decorated His creation with a dusting of snow and tipped the trees with shimmering icicles. All of nature looked as if it were dressed for a wedding ceremony. I was sure God had done this especially for me. Ice-laden trees bowed their branches all along the highway as if to sing, "Here comes the bride."

It was one of those Southern days that couldn't decide if it was the end of winter or the beginning of spring. As the day wore on, the bright sun warmed the earth to melt the snow and de-ice the trees. However, by nightfall, the temperature began to drop.

Steve and I headed back to school about seven o'clock that night. Just fifteen miles from the university, we approached a steep incline. We didn't realize that the downhill side of the road was covered with a sheet of ice.

As we began our descent, our car hit the thin veneer and began to spin out of control.

"Steve! We're going straight for that car," I cried as we headed directly into a set of oncoming headlights.

Seeing there was nothing he could do, Steve took his hands off the steering wheel and cried out, "Oh, God! Help us!"

One second we were headed directly toward an oncoming car. The next we were sitting off the side of the road in a ditch, facing in the opposite direction. Our bodies were pinned safely back into our seats. We did not have on seat belts.

"How did we miss that car?" I asked. "Where did it go? How did we get in this ditch?"

Shaken, Steve simply replied, "There's only one answer to those questions: God."

My mind immediately thought of Elisha and God's heavenly army of protecting angels. Elisha was an Old Testament prophet who warned Israel every time their nemesis, the king of Aram, was about to attack. The king was enraged and demanded to know the informant's identity. How did Israel always know what he was about to do before he did it?

"Elisha, the prophet who is in Israel, tells the king of Israel the very words you speak in your bedroom," the king's officers told him (2 Kings 6:12). So the king sent out an army of men to capture him. Listen to what happened when Elisha's servant woke up the next morning and saw the king's vast army surrounding them.

When the servant of the man of God got up and went out early the next morning, an army with horses and chariots had surrounded the city. "Oh no, my lord! What shall we do?" the servant asked.

"Don't be afraid," the prophet answered. "Those who are with us are more than those who are with them."

And Elisha prayed, "Open his eyes, LORD, so that he may see." Then the LORD opened the servant's eyes, and he looked and saw the hills full of horses and chariots of fire all around Elisha. (verses 15–17)

When God lifted the veil that separates the visible from the invisible, Elisha's servant caught a glimpse of the heavenly host that stood armed and ready to protect them. And those same angels are protecting God's children today.

In the natural scheme of things, there is no way Steve and I could have avoided a head-on collision with the other car that night. But I believe there was nothing "natural" about the incident. It was the *super*natural protection of God that reached down from heaven, picked up our spinning car, and gently set us off the side of the road facing backward. If we had landed in the ditch facing forward, the sheer impact of the sudden stop would have ricocheted our bodies through the windshield. No, there was nothing natural about any of this.

When I was a little girl, I used to sing the endless verses of "He's Got the Whole World in His Hands." Lines like, "He's got the ittybitty babies in His hands, He's got my momma and my papa in His hands, He's got my brothers and my sisters in His hands," and on it goes. On that frigid February night, over thirty years ago, I added a new verse for that song: "He's got me and Steve in His hands."

And here's a verse I'm singing today: "He's got you and me, sister, in His hands." I don't know of any other place I'd rather be. And in that you can place your trust.

Let's Pray

Dear Father, thank You for protecting me. Thank You for the angels that You assign to watch over me. I can be at peace today knowing that my very life is in Your hands. In Jesus's name, amen.

3

The Trust Fall

Gwen Smith

Today's Truth

When I am afraid, I will put my trust in you. (Psalm 56:3, NLT)

Friend to Friend

Our arms were braided across each other's, and our hands were locked tightly. As the young girl stood on the tall tree stump above us, she looked over her shoulder and saw with her own eyes that our formation was tight, that we were ready for her. She heard with her ears that we would catch her, that we would not let her get hurt. Yet the fear that screamed in her head told her not to do it. Not to fall backward.

Her legs shook and her lips quivered. Other campers had gone before her, and her cabinmates had successfully caught each one. But this camper hesitated—allowing the looming possibilities of failure and pain to paralyze her from action. The risks just seemed too great.

She trembled.

We encouraged.

She cried.

We encouraged.

Then, finally, with determination in her heart, she took the plunge. She fell straight backward onto the safety net of our arms. We bent low to the ground, giving way to her fall, and caught her with cheers of excitement. She did it! As her trembling legs regained their confidence, she stood tall and beamed from ear to ear—realizing that she had faced her fear. Joy was felt from heart to heart as each of us rejoiced with her.

Mission accomplished!

Early in the day, we had trekked across the campgrounds to the trust-fall station as a group of counselors and campers who didn't have a shared experience among us; we were an unconnected strand of strangers. Now our wooded team-building time had come to an end, and we left the trust-fall station having bonded deeply as a group of new girlfriends prepared for a fresh journey of fun and adventure.

Each of us took turns at the trust fall that day. We all faced that same set of scary circumstances and were forced to work through our doubts, tremblings, and fears. As a result, we learned valuable lessons and strengthened our relationships with one another.

Since my days of being a camp counselor, I've faced many scary trust falls in life: financial trials, relationship strains, relocations, sick loved ones, and difficult family matters. I've trembled and I've cried. I've been paralyzed by what-ifs and whys. We all go through difficult seasons and trials, times when we want to *see* the invisible arms of the One who says He will catch us, times when we are afraid to fall into them.

Wherever we go and whatever we face, God is with us—yesterday, today, and forever. He bids us to "live by faith, not by sight" (2 Corinthians 5:7). He wants us to trust Him. He catches us when we trust fall, when we live by faith. And to encourage us along the way, He spurs us on by sending a cloud of witnesses who testify of His

faithfulness. "Therefore, since we are surrounded by such a great cloud of witnesses, let us throw off everything that hinders and the sin that so easily entangles. And let us run with perseverance the race marked out for us" (Hebrews 12:1).

Today, whether you identify with the shaky young camper on the trust-fall stump or with the cabinmates who were filled with encouragement for her, God wants you to trust Him…right where you are. It might be scary. Tears might be shed. But God is faithful and can be trusted.

Like the psalmist, let's choose to say, "When I am afraid, I will put my trust in you. I praise God for what he has promised. I trust in God, so why should I be afraid?" (Psalm 56:3–4, NLT).

When we trust fall from our struggles into the faithful arms of God, we are freed from the fears that paralyze us. Trust Him today, friend. A great cloud of Girlfriends in God witnesses is cheering for you!

Let's Pray

Dear Lord, You are good, loving, and faithful—and You know exactly what I'm facing. Please take the burdens of my heart from me. Help me today to fall into a deeper place of trusting You. In Jesus's name I pray, amen.

A Father's Strong Arm

Sharon Jaynes

Today's Truth

Surely the arm of the LORD is not too short to save, nor his ear too dull to hear. (Isaiah 59:1)

Friend to Friend

The current was swift and fierce. I could feel my body being swept away like a hollow reed.

I was just a wisp of a girl—a six-year-old, forty-pound monkey with gangly arms and legs who vowed she could do anything her eleven-year-old mischievous brother, Stewart, could do. Standing on the glistening sand of Bogue Inlet, North Carolina, I hungrily watched as Stewart and his friend Jeffery plunged into the briny waters at the end of the island where the Atlantic Ocean merged with the Intracoastal Waterway. Stewart and Jeffery had one goal: to swim across the treacherous waters to a beckoning sandbar some one hundred feet away.

This was the spot at the end of the island where waves gave way to calm, salt water gave way to fresh, and sand gave way to soil. What looked like tranquil water on the surface was in reality a strong

undercurrent that sucked the ocean away from its home and toward the fresh water. Like a lovesick puppy mourning its master's departure down the driveway, I watched as the boys dived into the water and swam away from shore.

"I want to go too!" I called out after them.

"You're just a kid!" Stewart yelled back. "You stay there! You can't come!"

"It's not fair," I stormed. "He gets to do everything!"

"You stay here with us," my dad instructed. "You're too little. It's not safe."

My dad's remarks only made me even more determined to prove them all wrong. "If he can do it, I can do it," I mumbled. "I always get left behind."

When my dad turned his back to talk to a friend, I saw my chance and jumped into the water. My thin limbs were no match for the sucking force of the undertow and the pull of the swift current. Very quickly, my lithe body was swept away along with the ocean's salt, sand, and silt toward the fresh water. My salty tears mixed with the briny water, and my small cries for help went unheard. The strong ropes of current continued to pull me away from my family as they grew smaller on the shore.

Dad turned from his conversation to see that the boys had almost hit their mark. Out of the corner of his eye, he noticed small splashes to his far right. "Oh no!" he cried. "That's Sharon out there!"

My father dived into the water and cut through the menacing current. Propelled by panic, he reached me in a matter of moments. Like a fisherman's hook, Dad reached out his strong arm, grabbed my flailing body, and reeled me to his side. With one arm, he fought the current and pulled us safely to shore. My dad had rescued me. We both cried.

Have you ever been in a similar situation? Perhaps you've jumped into deep waters or strong currents that appeared benignly calm on the surface but turned malignantly deadly below. Perhaps you envied others who were headed in a certain direction and felt you were missing all the fun.

"Don't go there," your heavenly Father warned. "It's not safe."

"But why do they get to have all the fun?" you whined. "I always get left behind."

Then, when you thought God wasn't looking, in you jumped! Before you knew it, you were being swept away in the current of poor choices, sucked down by the undertow of self-centeredness, and pulled away as your family grew strangely small.

Oh, friend, my earthly father pulled me safely to shore that day when I was six years old, but my heavenly Father has pulled me safely to shore more times than I can count. When we ignore our Father's warnings, we forfeit the safety of His shore and plunge into the ocean of harm's way: the undertow of over-commitment, the current of wrong choices, and the rising tide of moral danger. Perhaps that's where you are right now. If so, there is hope. You only have to call out to God for help and He will pull you safely to shore. David cried out, "Turn your ear to me, come quickly to my rescue; be my rock of refuge, a strong fortress to save me" (Psalm 31:2) and "Reach down your hand from on high; deliver me and rescue me from the mighty waters" (Psalm 144:7).

"But, Sharon," you might say, "you don't know how far I've fallen. You don't know what a mess I've made of my life."

You are right. I don't know. But God does—and there is no place that you can go where His arm is too short to reach down and save you. That's a promise.

Call out to Him today. He's waiting.

Let's Pray

Dear heavenly Father, I am so glad that Your arm is never too short to save me, to pull me out of the difficult places of life. Forgive me for ignoring the Holy Spirit's warnings and jumping into treacherous waters that I should have avoided. Give me the strength to walk away when I feel that check in my spirit that says, "Don't go there." I love You, Lord, and I thank You for being my Rescuer, my Rock, and my Redeemer. In Jesus's name, amen.

5

The Perfect Storm

Mary Southerland

Today's Truth

LORD, you are my strength and my protection, my safe place in times of trouble. (Jeremiah 16:19, NCV)

Friend to Friend

I enjoy movies that have a happy ending. My family constantly teases me about my surreal perspective of movie entertainment, but honestly, life holds enough reality. Why would I want to pay good money to see even more reality made bigger and more frightening on a gigantic movie screen?

When the movie *The Perfect Storm* was first released, the previews suggested it had a happy ending. I should have known better, but we love the water and, really, how bad could it be?

We bought tickets, popcorn, and drinks, found the best seats in the theater, and prepared to be entertained. Wrong! Every scene showed tiny boats caught in the grip of frightening waves and fierce winds. I kept waiting for the storm to die down so everyone could go home with a boat full of fish to their anxious families who were confidently waiting for them on dry land.

Crash!

Another monstrous wave belted the boat and crew. By the end of the movie, I never wanted to set foot on a boat again, and I was worn out from trying to get everyone home where they would live happily ever after. I was tempted to demand a refund because of false advertising. Believe me, there was definitely no happy ending, but I did come away with a new fascination and deep respect for the sea.

I have a friend who loves to sail. When I asked him if he had ever been caught in a bad storm, he responded, "Many times!" I shook my head in disbelief, concluding that my friend was obviously a glutton for punishment. Of course I had to ask, "Then why on earth do you keep sailing?"

His answer was profound. "Mary, every sailor knows that there will be storms. You just learn what to do when the storm hits. In a severe storm, there is only one thing to do and only one way to survive. You have to put the ship in a certain position and keep her there."

The same is true in our lives. When the fierce storms of life overwhelm us, there is only one thing to do if we want to survive. We must position ourselves in the right place—in the hands of God—and He will keep us there until the storm has passed.

The words of the psalmist are filled with confidence and hope when he writes, "He stilled the storm to a whisper; the waves of the sea were hushed" (Psalm 107:29). We really can trust God to bring peace and to reduce the fiercest storm to a mere whisper. The faithful provision and sustaining comfort of God at work in our lives depends on the character and heart of God and our willingness to trust Him.

I love my children with all of my heart. Naturally, there are times when they make me very angry. They make wrong choices and sometimes even disappoint me, but if they are hurt, sick, or in trou-

ble, the anger, disappointment, and even disobedience are overruled by my love for them and a driving need to comfort them. If my imperfect heart responds to my imperfect children that way, think about how the perfect heart of our heavenly Father responds to us.

Richard Fuller, a nineteenth-century preacher, wrote:

> This, Christian, is what you must do. Sometimes, like Paul, you can see neither sun nor stars, and no small tempest lies on you. Reason cannot help you. Past experiences give you no light. Only a single course is left. You must stay upon the Lord; and come what may—winds, waves, cross seas, thunder, lightning, frowning rocks, roaring breakers—no matter what, you must lash yourself to the helm and hold fast your confidence in God's faithfulness and his everlasting love in Christ Jesus.

We can face every storm with confidence, knowing that God will redeem it for good. We can trust few things in this life, but God's faithfulness is one of them. When the hard times come and the storms roll in, trust God and hold on. He is with you.

Let's Pray

Father, thank You for Your faithfulness in my life. Forgive me when I let fear and doubt take over my heart and mind instead of choosing to trust You. Give me eyes to see the treasure buried at the heart of every storm and help me to choose trust even when I don't understand what You are doing in my life. Teach me, Lord. Let my life be an illustration of Your strength perfected in my weakness. In Jesus's name, amen.

Now It's Your Turn

TIME FOR REFLECTION

- Like in the story of Mary's precious granddaughter, Lelia, if you were to "bail on God," what would it look like?
- When you "trust-bail" on God now, which of the following best represents your style?

  A. I simply don't trust Him—I don't know how to—so I don't bother bailing.

  B. I look Him in the eyes, but I cling tightly to His God-shirt. I only fall back an arm's length…because although I *want* to trust Him, I struggle with trusting Him.

  C. I know He's strong and can handle the weight of my fall, but I bail cautiously just in case He's not interested in catching me this time.

  D. My eyes sparkle and connect with God's as I confidently fall backward and swing myself into the thick of circumstances, laughing at the days to come and trusting His strength to hold me.

- Which of the previous responses would you *like* to be true of you? What would it take to get you there? Are you willing to do those things?

- Can you think of a time when you recently trust-bailed on God and allowed His peace to hold you in spite of your challenge?

- Psalm 20:7 says, "Some trust in chariots and some in horses, but we trust in the name of the LORD our God." In your own words, describe the "chariots" and "horses" in your life. Where do you place your trust? In whom or what do you trust? Are you satisfied with the results?

- The New Century Version of the Bible translates today's key verse in Proverbs 3:5 as "Trust the Lord with all your heart, and don't depend on your own understanding." What part does human understanding play in the process of strengthening our faith in God?

- What does the word *all* mean to you when it comes to trusting God "with all your heart"?

- The realm of unseen things is mysterious, and God's sovereignty is beyond our understanding. We each face complicated, sometimes disappointing, situations, and hard life questions beg to be asked: If God has given angels charge over us, then why are some people protected in a car crash, but others aren't? If God really loves me, then why did He let *this* or *that* happen? Why didn't He deliver *my* loved one from cancer…from the accident… from temptation?

- There are times when God protects us from harm and times when He allows harm to touch us. There are times when we may have more questions than answers. This is hard stuff. What do you do with your unanswered heart-questions? Take a few

moments to share with one another or journal…and then pray for God to help you sift through the ashes of disappointment and see His unseen hope.

- Have you ever experienced the intervention of God in a way that left you shaken? How has this affected the way you trust Him?

- Do you think it's risky to trust God? Why or why not?

- Read Hebrews 12:12: "So take a new grip with your tired hands and stand firm on your shaky legs" (NLT, 1996 edition). What does it mean in your life to "take a new grip" and "stand firm" even on shaky legs?

- A trust fall is a relationship-building exercise where a person falls backward and relies on the other members of the group to catch them. Consider where you are in life with friendships right now. Who would you trust to catch you? Are you more often the friend on the tall stump needing to trust or the friend on the ground encouraging another to trust?

- It is so important for us girlfriends to rejoice with one another. Is there a way that God has nudged your heart closer toward trusting Him lately? Have you felt freed up to trust Him this week more than you have in the past? Throw down a happy dance with us as you journal about it or share with your coffee GiG or GiG group about it. Then share with us on the "Trusting God" page of our GiG website (www.GirlfriendsInGod .com/TrustingGod) or on our Facebook page (www.Facebook .com/GirlfriendsInGod). We love to throw down a good happy dance!

- Wrap up your response time with prayer. Move from confession to adoration to thanksgiving, and end with your petitions (personal prayer needs).

YOUR GIG TRUST ADVENTURE JOURNAL

Spend a few moments contemplating and journaling about some of the scriptural truths that moved your heart as you read the devotions this week. Then write a prayer of response to God.

_____

_____

_____

_____

_____

_____

_____

_____

_____

_____

_____

_____

_____

_____

_____

_____

_____

Therefore, since we are surrounded by such a great cloud of witnesses, let us throw off everything that hinders and the sin that so easily entangles. And let us run with perseverance the race marked out for us. (Hebrews 12:1)

1

May She Rest in Peace

Mary Southerland

Today's Truth

You, Lord, give true peace. You give peace to those who depend on you. You give peace to those who trust you. So, trust the Lord always. Trust the Lord because he is our Rock forever. (Isaiah 26:3–4, ICB)

Friend to Friend

We often associate the phrase "rest in peace" with death and the loss of a loved one. In fact, these words of comfort are often spoken at funerals or are included in the inscription on many headstones. Today, though, I want us to associate the words "rest in peace" with life instead of death.

Yes, God sent His Son, Jesus Christ, to die for our sin so that we can rest in peace when we die, but God also gave His one and only Son so that we can rest in peace every minute of every day. Does that sound like your life? Are you quick to trust God instead of worrying? Would the people who know you best describe you as a peaceful person? As I ask myself that question, the words *not so much* come to mind.

The Mayo Clinic once reported that the illnesses in 80 to 85

percent of their caseloads were caused by stress. An article titled "Is Stress the Cause of All Disease?" and printed in a leading medical journal said that until the beginning of the century, bacteria were the leading cause of illness. Not anymore. Stress is.

We all long for an inner calm—especially when we're in the valleys of life. We all want, pray for, and pursue peace. At the point of desperation, some people pursue peace by numbing their pain with alcohol, drugs, sex, food, success… The list is endless. Remember the old country song that says we are looking for love in all the wrong places and in too many faces? The same can be said about peace.

Some people tend to believe that peace is simply the absence of problems, valleys, and trials. Not so! Peace is a calm confidence that the Lord of the mountains is still on the throne—no matter how deep the valley may be. Peace recognizes Jesus walking on the water as He calms the crashing waves and stills the howling winds in your life. Trials become opportunities to trust God when peace reigns in a heart. That kind of peace can be found only in God.

Notice that I did not say we can find peace in church membership, in doing good things, in giving large sums of money to a charity or ministry, or even in being a really good person. Peace is a gift. When we enter into a personal relationship with Jesus Christ, we enter into true peace. Romans 5:1 says, "Since we have been made right with God by our faith, we have peace with God. This happened through our Lord Jesus Christ" (NCV).

We cannot bargain for or earn peace, girlfriend, but we will experience peace when we are willing to move away from our sin and turn to the Prince of Peace, Jesus Christ. Then, and only then, will we find rest in Him. Do you long for just one minute of peace? Don't settle. God offers a lifetime of peace if we are willing to trust Him.

I know the burden of life's trials can be heavy. I understand that

the problems we deal with every single day can weigh us down, but I also know that every problem can be given to God. When we surrender the weight of our trials and pain to Him, we will experience peace. As we allow God to carry the weight of our worry, the burden of our anxiety, and the penalty of every sin in our lives, peace will reign, leaving absolutely no room for the deadly trap of stress. Today, girlfriend, I pray that you will trust God and rest in peace.

Let's Pray

Father, this valley seems so deep and so dark. By faith, I choose to trust You as my Shepherd. Father, when I am tired, please carry me. I cannot see what is ahead. Will You guide me? I am often discouraged and ready to quit. Will You be my strength? I love You and want to please You with my life. Empower me to be all You created me to be. In Jesus's name, amen.

Finding Strength in Life's Fire Swamps

Gwen Smith

Today's Truth

Even youths grow tired and weary, and young men stumble and fall; but those who hope in the LORD will renew their strength. (Isaiah 40:30–31)

Friend to Friend

There is a scene in the whimsical and quirky film *The Princess Bride* in which some bad guys chase the two main characters, Princess Buttercup and Westley. In order to escape, Buttercup and Westley run into the treacherous Fire Swamp. (Insert scary music and experience creepy feelings here.)

The Fire Swamp presents three challenges: fire spurts, quicksand, and the R.O.U.S.—Rodents Of Unusual Size (stay with me...). At one point in the Fire Swamp adventure, Princess Buttercup falls into a pit of dry quicksand, instantly vanishing. Her brave hero, Westley, quickly grabs a sturdy vine and then plunges in to save his true love. Moments later both characters emerge from the

quicksand, gasping for breath, stunned by the events that have just taken place.

Stress can clutter our lives, consume us, just as fast and leave us gasping for breath, stunned, just as Buttercup and Westley were. When we find ourselves in the fire swamps of life, we ask question after question: *How did this happen? How did I get here? How do I get out of this scary place? Does anyone even know I'm in this pit? Who will be my hero?*

Falling into the quicksand of situational fire swamps becomes a greater risk when our souls are running on empty. Without a doubt, I'm more vulnerable on the days when my schedule is so full that my God-time is minimized. You probably know what it feels like to have a day filled with activity but a heart filled with emptiness. I imagine that you too feel at times as if all you do is work, work, work and give, give, give. You feel lonely in crowds of people and wonder if anyone really sees you or if anyone really cares. At times we all have too many obligations, too much stress, and not enough strength.

In order to survive these pitfalls, we must place our trust in God, the One who never grows tired or weary. He has strength readily available for us, and He knows where to direct our steps.

> He gives strength to the weary
>> and increases the power of the weak.
> Even youths grow tired and weary,
>> and young men stumble and fall;
> but those who hope in the LORD
>> will renew their strength.
> They will soar on wings like eagles;
>> they will run and not grow weary,
>> they will walk and not be faint. (Isaiah 40:29–31)

King David said it like this:

I waited patiently for the LORD;
    he turned to me and heard my cry.
He lifted me out of the slimy pit,
    out of the mud and mire;
he set my feet on a rock
    and gave me a firm place to stand.
He put a new song in my mouth,
    a hymn of praise to our God. (Psalm 40:1–3)

Stress happens. Fire swamps of life come and go. There's really no avoiding them. We can, however, be spiritually prepared to face their challenges. God equips us—strengthens us—as we wait on Him. As we trust in Him. As we dwell with Him.

Have you refueled in His presence lately? Take time to meet with God one on one today. As the psalmist wrote, "Let us go to his dwelling place, let us worship at his footstool, saying, 'Arise, LORD, and come to your resting place, you and the ark of your might'" (Psalm 132:7–8).

Friend, keep company with Him today. All day. When you do, you will experience His strength for each moment and His direction in each challenge. You will increase in your faith. Oswald Chambers, prominent minister, teacher, and author of *My Utmost for His Highest*, had this to say: "At the most unexpected moments in your life there is a whisper of the Lord, 'Come to Me,' and you are immediately drawn to Him. Personal contact with Jesus changes everything."

The journey to becoming a God-strong, Jesus-trusting woman is all about personal contact with Jesus. You and I will experience

greater peace and deeper faith as we determine to respond to His constant invitation to come. But don't worry—Jesus is no stranger to stress. He walked the same earth we do and dealt with the struggles and strains we deal with. He loved many a stressed-out woman while here on earth and many more before and since His ascension. He knows your stresses, your fire swamps, your distractions, your "stuff," and He invites you to come to Him just the same. Just as you are.

When we position ourselves in the presence of the Peace Giver and look to Him to lead and prioritize our heart matters, the strengthening begins. So take time to consider your priorities, evaluate your online activities, and determine what life clutter needs to stay and what needs to go. Examine your heart, your exhaustion, and the pains of your yesterdays. Take an honest and possibly uncomfortable look at the material, emotional, social, and relationship clutter that keeps you from the freedom that God intends for you to experience. Then, once you eliminate what you don't need, renew and rejuvenate your soul space with what you do need: spiritual disciplines like a daily quiet time, personal worship, and God's Word.

Are you ready? Ready to move to a fresh place of soul rest and spirit strength through fully trusting God? Ready to simplify your faith and press on to become the woman that Jesus is really calling you to be?

I know I am.

Let the strengthening begin.

Let's Pray

Heavenly Father, You are my Strong Tower, my Deliverer, and my Shelter. I'm running to You now. Please renew my strength, refresh my faith, and lead me with Your Holy Spirit as You guide me through my day. In Jesus's name I pray, amen.

Consider the Puppies

Sharon Jaynes

Today's Truth

Consider how the wild flowers grow. They do not labor or spin. Yet I tell you, not even Solomon in all his splendor was dressed like one of these. (Luke 12:27)

Friend to Friend

When our golden retriever was three years old, we decided to let her "get married" and have puppies. After making sure she was indeed pregnant, I read up on animal husbandry just in case I needed to help her out. The puppy book had some very interesting instructions. One idea was to procure a child-sized plastic swimming pool and line it with newspapers. When it was time for the dog to go into labor, the book assured me, Ginger would step into the pool, begin to shred the papers, and form a nest of sorts. I thought this was the most ridiculous thing I had ever read. I mean, who was going to tell Ginger to step into the birthing pool? And how was she going to know to start shredding newspaper, for goodness' sake?

I don't know what possessed me, but I did what the book said. I remember going through the checkout line at Wal-Mart.

"This pool here for your little ones?" the cashier asked cheerfully.

"Ah, no. It's for my dog to have puppies in," I explained.

"I see," the cashier replied as she refused to make further eye contact.

I took the swimming pool home and lined it with newspapers, just as the book said. I also gathered the suggested operating room equipment: scissors and dental floss in case she didn't cut the cord herself, a heating pad in a box to serve as an incubator if needed, and a bulb syringe to aspirate a puppy's mouth and nose if it wasn't breathing properly.

A few days later I heard a strange sound. When I opened the garage door, I saw Ginger in the swimming pool, shredding paper!

"God," I prayed, "I don't know if it's acceptable to pray for a dog, but please tell her what to do so I don't have to."

After Ginger panted and shredded for two hours, she gave one big push and out came puppy number one. Ginger didn't see junior lying under her bushy tail, and she just looked at me wild-eyed as if to say, "What in the world was that!"

Looking over at the scissors and dental floss, I prayed again. "Lord, tell her what to do." With the umbilical cord still attached, I pulled the seemingly lifeless wet wee-wums around so Ginger could see him.

"Look, Ginger. This is what's happening. Don't you know what to do?"

Ginger took one look at that wet, mousy-looking creature and sprang into action like a skilled physician. She chewed the umbilical

cord to a half inch from the puppy's tummy (just like the book had instructed me to do) and then began licking life into its motionless body like a doctor giving a baby those first swats on the behind. In just a few minutes, Fletcher, her firstborn, was scootching around the pool, rooting for his mother's milk. Once again, she knew exactly what to do. Satisfied, she looked up at me and smiled. (Well, it looked like a smile to me.)

About two hours later, she started the familiar panting again, and shortly puppy number two came into the world. This time I didn't have to pull the pup around. Ginger followed standard procedure on her own. When number three came onto the scene, there was a little problem. This pup was still in the amniotic sac, floating like a rag doll in a Ziploc baggie. I was stunned, but not Ginger! Again, she knew exactly what was needed. She chewed a hole in the sac and pulled the puppy out. When she saw it wasn't breathing, she licked more vigorously than before until the pup started breathing on its own.

For six hours, I watched in amazement as Ginger performed one miraculous feat after another. Well, to me it was miraculous, but some people just call it instinct. I've always disliked that word *instinct*. It implies that it is something that just automatically exists in animals, but my question is, who put the instinct there? When it comes to having babies, we humans read books, go to classes, and have a host of doctors and nurses at our sides. But think of all of God's creatures that He cares for everyday that know exactly what to do when the time comes.

Watching the delivery of Ginger's puppies birthed in me a whole new appreciation of the love and care that God has for all of His creation. And if He cares for the creeping, crawling, flying critters of

creation, how much more will He care for His children, who are created in His own image? Jesus explained:

> Consider how the wild flowers grow. They do not labor or
> spin. Yet I tell you, not even Solomon in all his splendor was
> dressed like one of these. If that is how God clothes the grass
> of the field, which is here today, and tomorrow is thrown into
> the fire, how much more will he clothe you—you of little
> faith!… But seek his kingdom, and these things will be given
> to you as well. (Luke 12:27–28, 31)

Today, pay attention to all the ways that God is taking care of your needs and look for His fingerprints on the moments of your day.

Let's Pray
Dear Creator of all things great and small, how I marvel at Your handiwork. I praise You for the majesty of the mountains and the minuteness of a flea. I stand in awe of Your creation and thank You for allowing me to be a small part of it. In Jesus's name, amen.

Always on Time

Mary Southerland

Today's Truth

And my God will meet all your needs according to the riches of his glory in Christ Jesus. (Philippians 4:19)

Friend to Friend

I grew up in Texas, where we lived in what some might call a shack on the edge of a small town. To me, it was just home. My father died when I was four years old, and my amazing mother often worked three jobs to make ends meet—a meeting that did not always happen. However, looking back, I can honestly say that God always provided what we needed—when we needed it.

He still does.

My husband and I knew the finances would be tight, but we did not expect the brakes to go out on one of our cars, and we certainly didn't plan a trip to urgent care or imagine that the electric bill would be so high all in the same month. The cost of groceries suggested that we fast for a while—and the rent was due. A quick glance at our bank account assured me that the numbers had not magically changed

overnight. We simply did not have enough money to pay our bills. I know that many of you can relate.

You would think that after years and years of serving God, I would know and walk in the truth that God is our Source and that He provides everything we need—when we need it. Oh no! I went from faith to fear in a matter of minutes. Panic set in as a frantic search for some solution to our financial problems ensued. In the midst of that panic, I suddenly remembered the mail. Interesting timing, wasn't it?

Since I had not checked the mail in three days, I expected the box to be crammed full. It was. In fact, I could see corners of envelopes sticking out of the mail slot. Faith whispered, "Maybe those envelopes are filled with checks." Doubt shouted, "Get real! Every single envelope is a demand for money you do not have." There was only one way to find out. When I unlocked the mailbox, an avalanche of newspapers, envelopes, cards, and magazines spilled into my hands and onto the ground. The mailman had also left me a key to the larger mailbox below that was usually reserved for packages. It was full of mail as well. I cleared off the kitchen table where I began sorting through the mound of paper, discarding all of the junk mail and arranging the bills according to their due dates. It was not an encouraging process, as the stack of bills grew tall at an alarming rate.

And then I saw it—an envelope that seemed to stand out from the rest. A sliver of excitement worked its way into my doubting heart as I slowly opened the envelope. The return address told me it was from the women's ministry director of a church where I had spoken several months before. One of my best friends was a member of the church, and I had offered to speak for an event that I hoped would encourage her and help their new women's ministry get off the

ground. I did not ask for or expect an honorarium, but as I slowly opened the envelope, I saw a check written for the exact amount that would meet our financial needs for the month.

I literally collapsed in a kitchen chair and began to pray, asking God to forgive my lack of faith and my choice to worry instead of trusting Him. I marveled in the knowledge that the check had been written long before the need became evident to me. In other words, God met our need before we even knew we *had* a need.

God's love is not a shallow love that always rescues us easily or quickly. God loves us enough to walk us through the fiery times that make us more like His Son, Jesus Christ. His ways are not our ways, and our thoughts are so often very different from His thoughts. God is holy. He is faithful. And we really can trust Him to work at the right time and in the right way for our good and His glory.

By the way, I am a mail freak and have been for most of my life. I usually check the mail every single day without fail. Not that particular week! God knew I needed a reminder of His faithfulness and He knew exactly when I needed it…and He was right on time.

Let's Pray
Father, thank You for meeting the needs in my life in Your perfect timing. Forgive me when I fail to trust You and instead allow worry to steal my joy. I want to be patient and learn how to wait on You to work in my life. Your faithfulness sustains me and Your mercy blesses my life. I praise You, God! In Jesus's name, amen.

5

Holding Fast to the Faithful One

Gwen Smith

Today's Truth

But we have this treasure in jars of clay to show that this all-surpassing power is from God and not from us. We are hard pressed on every side, but not crushed; perplexed, but not in despair; persecuted, but not abandoned; struck down, but not destroyed. (2 Corinthians 4:7–9)

Friend to Friend

My husband and I were in a waiting period. His company had gone through a merger and was collapsing positions and territories, which left his employment in jeopardy. For months we didn't know if Brad would keep his job or if he would need to look for another one. During that time, God bid us to trust Him.

Choosing to trust God is so daily, isn't it? When I looked only at the what-ifs of Brad's job situation—the possible unemployment, the grueling process of job hunting, the financial strain unemployment would bring, and the uncertainty of the economy—my faith and

God-confidence shook and waned. Fear and doubt knocked on my heart, suitcases in hand, wanting to move in and take up residence. On the other hand, when I fixed my eyes on God, considered His character, and remembered the ways He had brought us through hard times in the past, my faith was strengthened. Courage, confidence, and joy knocked on my heart! And they are much better residents!

The Old Testament book of Ruth features the heartwarming story of Ruth and Naomi, two women who faced difficult circumstances and an uncertain future. Following the death of her husband and sons, Naomi decided to move back to Israel, her homeland. Though she freed her daughters-in-law to stay in their home country of Moab and remarry, Ruth refused to leave Naomi's side.

Determined and loyal, Ruth held tightly to the mother-in-law she loved deeply and to the God of Israel, whom she now called her own. Though our natural tendency in hard times is often to try to go it alone, I've learned from Ruth—and from my own experience—that in turbulent times it's vital that we hold fast to our faithful God and to the ones we love.

> "Look," said Naomi, "your sister-in-law is going back to her people and her gods. Go back with her."
>
> But Ruth replied, "Don't urge me to leave you or to turn back from you. Where you go I will go, and where you stay I will stay. Your people will be my people and your God my God. Where you die I will die, and there I will be buried. May the LORD deal with me, be it ever so severely, if even death separates you and me." When Naomi realized that Ruth was determined to go with her, she stopped urging her. (Ruth 1:15–18)

God breathed hope into the souls of Naomi and Ruth through their kinsman-redeemer, Boaz. The book of Ruth goes on to tell the fascinating account of how God lovingly cared for and blessed Naomi, using the faithful friendship and kindness of Ruth to "renew [her] life and sustain [her]" (4:15). Naomi traveled back to Bethlehem as a broken, depressed, and hopeless widow, but she was comforted and restored by the loving hand of God.

Like Naomi, when I experience difficult times—like the one Brad and I were facing last fall—peace and strength surround me when I choose to trust God. Some days I choose well. Some days I don't. Choosing to trust is essential.

How can we choose to trust God? I've found that my courage to trust is bolstered by playing praise music, meditating on God's goodness, reading Scripture, and praying. Those things, collectively, renew my mind and strengthen my faith.

No matter what challenges you face today, take comfort in the truth that God knows every issue on your heart and is able to shoulder your burdens. Hold fast to the faithful One. Your challenges do not fall outside the scope of God's ability to intervene. God is mysterious, He's powerful, and He's able! When you lift your eyes from your situation and fix them on your Savior—when you choose to trust Him—you will find peace in the pain and strength in the struggle.

> Trust in the LORD with all your heart
>> And do not lean on your own understanding.
> In all your ways acknowledge Him,
>> And He will make your paths straight.
>>> (Proverbs 3:5–6, NASB)

Let's Pray

Holy Father, You know exactly where I am right now, and You know the circumstances of my life. Please give me the courage to be gracious in my relationships, and help me to trust You today. In Jesus's name, amen.

Now It's Your Turn

TIME FOR REFLECTION

- If you had a personal pressure gauge, what level would your stress-o-meter read?
  A. Cool as a cucumber. Got this rest-in-Christ-thing down. *"Trust-chillin'."*
  B. Teeter-tottery. Up and down between stress and peace. *"Doing my best to struggle well."*
  C. Overtaken by S.O.U.S.—Stresses of Unusual Size! *"Help! I've fallen into a fire-swampy life pit and I can't get up!"*

- What would you say your personal contact with Jesus is?
  A. Nonexistent beyond this book and discussion
  B. Monthly
  C. Weekly
  D. Daily
  E. Several times a day

- Do you think there is a direct correlation between the levels of peace you experience in life and the frequency of your contact with Jesus? Why or why not?

- Has God ever met a need that you had before you even *knew* you had a need? If yes, when? (We girls like scoop!)
- Read 2 Corinthians 4:7–9 and fill in the blanks of the statements below: "But we have this treasure in jars of clay to show that this all-surpassing power is from God and not from us. We are hard pressed on every side, but not crushed; perplexed, but not in despair; persecuted, but not abandoned; struck down, but not destroyed."

  As a believer in Christ (a jar of clay), I am and at times will be _____ ,

  _____ ,

  _____ , and

  _____ .

  As a daughter of the all-powerful, Mighty God, I am not and never will be _____ ,

  _____ ,

  _____ , or

  _____ .

  (Now give someone a high five and whoop it up!)

- There's an old saying that goes: "Stop telling God how big your mountain is and start telling that mountain how big your God is!" Sometimes we allow our mountains to do all the talking and all the boasting. Is there a mountain in your life that needs to be spiritually resized? If so, pause to pray about this right now.
- What helps to bolster your God-courage and increases your faith strength?
- Wrap up your response time with prayer. Move from confession, to adoration, to thanksgiving, and end with your petitions (personal prayer needs).

YOUR GIG TRUST ADVENTURE JOURNAL

Spend a few moments contemplating and journaling about some of the scriptural truths that moved your heart as you read the devotions this week. Then write a prayer of response to God.

_____

_____

_____

_____

_____

_____

_____

_____

_____

_____

_____

_____

_____

_____

_____

_____

_____

_____

_____

So we say with confidence, "The Lord is my helper; I will not be afraid. What can mere mortals do to me?" (Hebrews 13:6)

Jesus Loves Me

Sharon Jaynes

Today's Truth

Who shall separate us from the love of Christ? Shall trouble or hardship or persecution or famine or nakedness or danger or sword?... For I am convinced that neither death nor life, neither angels nor demons, neither the present nor the future, nor any powers, neither height nor depth, nor anything else in all creation, will be able to separate us from the love of God that is in Christ Jesus our Lord. (Romans 8:35, 38–39)

Friend to Friend

It was the first anniversary of the terrorist bombing of September 11, 2001. The rubble from the World Trade Center had been cleared and the Pentagon repaired, but men and women all across America still mourned the three thousand lives that were lost on that dark day in our country's history. In my hometown, a memorial was set up on an expanse of land: a sea of twelve-inch white crosses representing the men and women who had died.

Kathy and her family went to see the memorial, along with her

seventeen-year-old daughter, Heather, and her three-year-old niece, Taylor. It was difficult for young Taylor to understand exactly what was going on and why so many people were sad, but she obediently walked hand-in-hand with her cousin between the tiny crosses. At some point, little Taylor wandered away from her family, and no one seemed to notice.

It was reverently silent as the crowd of mourners looked at the names inscribed on the white memorials. Some crosses were decorated with flowers, others with teddy bears or other memorabilia. But nothing spoke of the pain and loss more poignantly than the silence broken by quiet sobs. *How did this happen? How would the shattered families piece their lives back together? How would life ever be the same?* These silent questions wafted between the crosses and wove throughout the very fabric of the entire country with threads of anger, mistrust, and pain.

Then, as if coming directly from heaven, a small voice floated on the breeze and broke the silence with sweetness. Every eye turned to notice a little girl with outstretched arms who was twirling in circles among the crosses.

With her face lifted toward the sky, Taylor was singing:

Jesus loves me! This I know
For the Bible tells me so.
Little ones to Him belong;
They are weak, but He is strong.
Yes, Jesus loves me!
Yes, Jesus loves me!
Yes, Jesus loves me!
The Bible tells me so.

Time seemed to stand still as hundreds of mourners turned their attention on one small girl with a big message. Even in the midst of pain, even with the loss of life, loss of dreams, and loss of hope… Jesus loves us.

In 2 Corinthians 4:6–9, 16–18 Paul reminds us:

For God, who said, "Let light shine out of darkness," made his light shine in our hearts to give us the light of the knowledge of God's glory displayed in the face of Christ. But we have this treasure in jars of clay to show that this all-surpassing power is from God and not from us. We are hard pressed on every side, but not crushed; perplexed, but not in despair; persecuted, but not abandoned; struck down, but not destroyed…. Therefore we do not lose heart. Though outwardly we are wasting away, yet inwardly we are being renewed day by day. For our light and momentary troubles are achieving for us an eternal glory that far out-weighs them all. So we fix our eyes not on what is seen, but on what is unseen, since what is seen is temporary, but what is unseen is eternal.

If ever there was a group of people who had felt deserted by God, it was Jesus's disciples. For three-and-a-half years they had walked with Jesus, experiencing His miracles and messages. They had wit-nessed His power in feeding five thousand men, plus women and children, with two loaves and five fishes. They had felt the waves beneath their tiny boat subside at His command. They had wit-nessed Him resurrect a lifeless child during a funeral procession, re-store the rotting flesh of a leper's limbs, render sight to a man blind

from birth, and release a man bound by demons. They had seen Him walk on water, outwit the Pharisees, and win the lost. But their hopes and dreams had died on that Roman cross and had been sealed away in a darkened tomb. However, three days later, as God rolled the stone away and Jesus walked out of that empty tomb, He fulfilled their dreams beyond anything they could have ever imagined. And that is the hope that gives us a firm place to stand when the very ground beneath seems to tremble in a quake of fear and doubt.

No matter what you are going through today, Jesus loves you... this I know. And in Him you can always put your trust.

Let's Pray

Jesus, thank You for loving me and for giving Your life for me. Thank You for the promise that nothing can ever separate me from that love. In Jesus's name, amen.

Just Like Your Father

Mary Southerland

Today's Truth

He will sit as a refiner and purifier of silver. (Malachi 3:3)

Friend to Friend

The story is told of a group of women who met each week to study the Bible, hoping to learn more about the nature and character of God and how He works in our lives. The women were puzzled and even a little troubled by the description of God they found in Malachi 3:3, "He will sit as a refiner and purifier of silver."

One of the women offered to do a little research on the subject and report back to the group at their next meeting. The woman found a local silversmith and made an appointment to observe him at work, explaining that she was particularly interested in the process of refining silver. She watched as the craftsman carefully selected a piece of silver for his demonstration. She thought the piece of silver was already beautiful, but evidently the silversmith saw something that she could not see. As he held the silver over the furnace, the craftsman explained that the silver had to be placed in the middle of

the fire where the flames were hottest so all of the impurities would be burned away.

The woman was silent for a moment as her thoughts drifted to the fiery trials she was facing in her own life. Honestly, she did not get it. *Why would a loving God allow His children to suffer when He could so easily deliver them? In fact, why does God even allow bad things to happen to people who are seeking Him and really trying to live for Him?*

The woman asked the silversmith if it was true that he had to sit in front of the fire the whole time the silver was being refined. "Oh yes!" he replied. "I cannot take my eyes off the silver. If it is left in the furnace even a moment too long, it will be destroyed." The woman suddenly understood the beauty and comfort of Malachi 3:3: "He will sit as a refiner and purifier of silver."

Yes, there are times when it seems as if we will be swallowed whole by the fires of hell itself. The pain seems too hard to bear. The fear is paralyzing. The doubt is overwhelming and the questions flood our hearts and minds.

Is God really who He says He is?

Will He really do what He says He will do?

Will He really keep His promises?

Can I really trust God?

Our trials are not random persecutions. Heaven is not in a panic. Where we are and what we are going through is no surprise to God. We may be knocked down and kicked around by life, but if we have a personal relationship with Jesus Christ, we will not be destroyed.

Our lives are often filled with excess baggage and waste, such as a cherished sin we refuse to relinquish or an addiction to which we are enslaved. At times our emotional garbage weighs us down or our unforgiving spirits hold us prisoner. Fiery trials come to burn away

the guilt of sin and then purify our hearts. From those ashes of freedom, the Father then creates a work of beauty.

I believe the words I just wrote.

I know and accept the truth that trials and hard times make me stronger and strengthen my faith, but honestly, there are times when I want it all to stop. I find myself asking, "How much is enough, Lord? How many trials do I have to endure? When will the pain and trouble end?"

"How do you know when the silver is fully refined?" the woman asked. The silversmith smiled and answered, "Oh, that's easy." The refining process is complete when I can see my image reflected in the silver."

God is not committed to our comfort; He is committed to our character. Only God can exchange the ashes of our sin for the beauty of His forgiveness and grace. God alone can replace our despair with His peace that passes all understanding. Hope can only be found in Him. Our purpose in life is to know and become more like Jesus... and to act just like our Father.

Let's Pray

Father, I want to be more like You. Give me the strength to withstand the trials in my life. Help me love the people who are hard to love and forgive the people who have hurt and even abused me. Burn away the sin in my life and empower me to live for You. Create a clean heart in me, Lord, and teach me how to trust You and live for You. In Jesus's name, amen.

The Broken Way

Gwen Smith

Today's Truth

Moses answered the people, "Do not be afraid. Stand firm and you will see the deliverance the LORD will bring you today.... The LORD will fight for you; you need only to be still." (Exodus 14:13–14)

Friend to Friend

While at my son's football game one day, I had a moving conversation with another team mom. It was the first time we'd ever dialogued beyond socially expected niceties. Between the cheers that went up for our football-playing boys, she stumbled upon the fact that I was a Jesus-loving girl. Excited to find out that I was a GiG, she began to share about how God has intimately drawn her heart to His over the past five years. How He met her where she was and ministered to her through the hands of others. How He sparked life into her soul through His Son Jesus Christ.

She was radiant.

She spoke with excitement, joy in every sentence, and praise on her tongue for the God who gives her strength and life. This dear

football mom opened her heart and told me of her grueling battle with an aggressive form of breast cancer.

She had been diagnosed with cancer at the age of thirty-five. A wife and mother to three small children, she initially was angry with God for allowing a disease to ravage her body...furious that her husband and children might have to live without her. Though my new friend fought to understand the why of it all, she confidently testified that God used the pain-filled journey on the broken road of cancer to lead her to saving grace. She is now grateful for the broken way that God breathed new life into her soul as she battled death in her body.

As she spoke, the troubles of my life faded to a humble corner of my heart. Her words reminded me that God really can and should be glorified through each hard place we find ourselves in. I was freshly reminded to trust God.

Life is filled with challenges. The struggles we endure often leave our hearts breaking and our minds aching for reprieve. I've not battled cancer, but I have experienced my fair share of times when I've been crushed by circumstances that are beyond my control—much like she was. As a wife, mother, daughter, and friend, I've learned that hard times are inevitable and that they hurt.

Toward the end of our conversation about her cancer and her faith, my new friend confided that fear still tries to invade her days. She said that she constantly has to choose faith and to trust God instead of dwelling on the possibilities of another future diagnosis. Every one of us doubts at times. We all fail to trust. But Scripture assures us that even when we are faithless, God remains faithful. As we walk broken paths that challenge our faith, the truth remains that God does deliver in and through the pain. Though there are

struggles that we might take to the grave with us, God is still good. Each hard place is an opportunity for Jesus to show His power in and through our lives.

When we find ourselves on the broken way, we often feel like we are wandering in the wilderness. In Exodus chapters 13–14, we see a dreary desert drama of the Israelites' wilderness wanderings. Stop here to read the full account now if you can.

> When Pharaoh let the people go, God did not lead them on
> the road through the Philistine country, though that was
> shorter. For God said, "If they face war, they might change
> their minds and return to Egypt." So God led the people
> around by the desert road toward the Red Sea. (13:17–18)

As God moved through the leadership of Moses to bring His people from captivity to freedom, from poverty to inheritance, He did not lead the Israelites the easy way. They didn't get to take the "paved" road—even though it was shorter. They had to walk through the desert. God led them the harder way because He knew it was best for them in the long run. Sometimes He leads us along the harder way too. The broken way. Even though our minds conceive an easier solution, God knows what is unknown to us, He sees what is unseen to us, and His ways are trustworthy and best.

> By day the LORD went ahead of them in a pillar of cloud to
> guide them on their way and by night in a pillar of fire to
> give them light, so that they could travel by day or night.
> Neither the pillar of cloud by day nor the pillar of fire by
> night left its place in front of the people....

Then the angel of God, who had been traveling in front of Israel's army, withdrew and went behind them. The pillar of cloud also moved from in front and stood behind them, coming between the armies of Egypt and Israel. Throughout the night the cloud brought darkness to the one side and light to the other side; so neither went near the other all night long.

Then Moses stretched out his hand over the sea, and all that night the LORD drove the sea back with a strong east wind and turned it into dry land. The waters were divided, and the Israelites went through the sea on dry ground, with a wall of water on their right and on their left." (Exodus 13:21–22; 14:19–22)

God has given us His Holy Spirit to lead us by day and by night, to be our Strength, our Power, and our Direction in the deserts of life. Just as God made a way for the Israelites when they called on Him as they faced a seemingly impossible Red Sea situation, God will make a way for you. Call on His name. Trust His plan. Reach for His hand.

Let's Pray

Dear Lord, forgive me for the times when I try to navigate the broken path of life on my own. When my heart is heavy with burdens, please give me Your strength and remind my soul to trust You. I need Your guidance and power today. In Jesus's name, amen.

Sometimes I Just Don't Get It

Mary Southerland

Today's Truth

As the heavens are higher than the earth, so are my ways higher than your ways and my thoughts than your thoughts. (Isaiah 55:9)

Friend to Friend

Sometimes I just don't get it. I have been a Christ-follower for many years. I am a Christian author and speaker and the women's ministry director at the church where my husband is the lead teaching pastor. Over the years, God has brought me out of more pits than I can count, and I have attended church since the day I was born. My faith in God should be unwavering, and I should never doubt or question Him or His plan. But sometimes I do.

I just received a phone call telling me that a young mother (whom we will call Sally) in our church was admitted to the hospital to have her baby after nine months of a very normal pregnancy with no complications. Sally and her husband should be celebrating the birth of their little girl, but instead they are planning her memorial

service. The baby died in the birth process, and Sally is in ICU after losing a lot of blood due to a torn uterus.

Sally is an extraordinary young woman who is well known for her sweet smile and kind heart. She directs our preschool ministry and helps her husband lead one of our fastest growing life groups. I don't get it! Why would God let this happen to *them*?

You may be offended by my next statement, but if I am brutally honest, my faulty human mind and sin-tainted heart can almost— *almost*—come to grips with such a horrific circumstance happening to someone who is evil and has turned their back on God. Bad things should happen to bad people, and good things should happen to good people. Sounds logical and fair, right?

But you and I both know that life is not fair and that our human logic is a shallow substitute for God's sovereignty. We are broken people living in a broken world. Bad things do happen to good people while those who mock God seem to prosper, and it's been that way for a long time. Take Job, for example.

> The LORD said to Satan, "Have you considered my servant Job? There is no one on earth like him; he is blameless and upright, a man who fears God and shuns evil."
>
> "Does Job fear God for nothing?" Satan replied. "Have you not put a hedge around him and his household and everything he has? You have blessed the work of his hands, so that his flocks and herds are spread throughout the land. But now stretch out your hand and strike everything he has, and he will surely curse you to your face."
>
> The LORD said to Satan, "Very well, then, everything he has is in your power, but on the man himself do not lay a finger." (Job 1:8–12)

Don't miss the important fact that God not only *allowed* Satan to test Job, but dictated *how* Satan could test him. Job went from having vast wealth to great poverty, losing everything he and his wife had, including their ten children. Job's wife urged her husband to turn away from God and curse Him, to forsake the very faith that had blessed her and Job for so long—but Job stood firm.

> "He fell to the ground in worship and said: "Naked I came
> from my mother's womb, and naked I will depart. The LORD
> gave and the LORD has taken away; may the name of the
> LORD be praised." (1:20–21)

Job was an extraordinary man, husband, father, and leader who served God faithfully. His faithfulness to God in prosperity was a powerful testimony, but his faithfulness to God in the face of death, pain, and despair was even more powerful. Did Job doubt and question God? Absolutely! Did Job openly and honestly grieve his loss and weep in his pain? Yes, but he remained faithful to God, even when he did not understand why God would let him endure such suffering and even when his heart and body were broken. God was pleased with Job and rewarded him for his faithfulness: "The LORD blessed the latter part of Job's life more than the former part" (42:12).

Sally's faith reminds me of Job and his faith. God is already using this tragedy for good. The nurses and doctors could not explain the extraordinary strength they saw in this young couple. Seekers were impacted by the love and prayer support that Sally and her family received from our church members. I have no doubt that this young couple will grow stronger in the Lord and that their faith will be a powerful testimony of God's grace, mercy, and love. We may not understand or like God's process, but we can trust His heart.

One day, all of our question marks will be yanked into exclamation points...and we will get it. Until then, we walk by faith and not by sight—trusting God.

Let's Pray

Father, I am so sorry for doubting You when life is hard. Forgive me for questioning Your plan when it seems to make no sense. I want to be a woman of faith who trusts You no matter what happens. Help me cultivate the kind of faith Job had and strengthen me for every trial ahead. Guard my mouth, Lord. Take my thoughts captive and make them Yours. Today, I choose faith over fear and trust over doubt. In Jesus's name, amen.

5

Would You Be Afraid?

Sharon Jaynes

Today's Truth

Why are you so afraid? Do you still have no faith? (Mark 4:40)

Friend to Friend

She was among an eager group of four-year-old children crowded around my feet as I taught their Sunday school lesson. They listened intently as I tried to paint them a mental picture of Jesus and His disciples trapped in a thunderstorm on the Sea of Galilee.

"One day Jesus was in a tiny fishing boat with twelve of His friends. While Jesus was taking a nap, a fierce storm rolled across the sky. The mighty winds bleeeeeeew and rocked the little boat back and forth, back and forth. The waves were soooooo big; they splashed over the sides of the boat and got the men all wet. Then water started to fill up the boat. And do you know what happens when a boat gets full of water?"

"It sinks," they chimed together.

"That's right." I continued with a concerned look on my face. "Also the lightning was soooooo bright, it looked like fire in the sky.

And the thunder was soooooo loud, they could feel it booming in their chests."

After painting this picture of impending doom, I thought my pint-size audience would be just a little worried about the fate of these men trapped in the storm. I asked the question: "Now, if you were in a tiny boat like theirs, caught in a terrible storm like this, would you be afraid?"

Then one precious little girl, confident and unshaken by the entire scenario, shrugged her shoulders and replied, "Not if Jesus was in the boat with me."

I will never forget that answer. As her words have echoed in my mind, I've come to realize that this is the answer that calms all my worries and fears. Just as the storm raged all around the disciples, many times the storms of life rage around me. A friend discovers she has cancer, a husband loses his job, a child is born with birth defects. These are storms with waves of emotion so high that our lifeboat fills with tears and appears that it could sink at any moment. Waves of fear rock our boat and threaten to spill us into the depths of despair—and we don't even have a life jacket to keep us afloat.

"Tell me, would you be afraid?"

"Not if Jesus was in the boat with me."

When the squall on the Sea of Galilee raged against the disciples' boat, Jesus was sound asleep. "Lord, save us! We're going to drown!" the frightened men cried.

"You of little faith," He replied. "Why are you so afraid?"

Now if I had been on that boat—I'll be honest—I would probably have shot back, "Are You kidding me? Look at these waves! We're doomed! There's no way we're going to make it safely to shore! How can You sleep through this? Don't You even care about us?"

Come to think of it, I have said those very words in a few storms of my own.

And what did Jesus do? He stood—stood and spoke to the world He created: "Silence! Quiet down! Be still!" And like a rowdy classroom of overactive children suddenly silenced by a teacher's authoritative command, the wind and the waves submitted to Jesus. The sea became smooth as glass and the wind but a whispering breeze.

The disciples were amazed. I am always amazed.

We will always have storms in our lives. Jesus promised us: "In this world you will have trouble. But take heart! I have overcome the world" (John 16:33).

So what am I going to do when the storms of life sweep in unexpectedly? As my little pupil taught so eloquently that day, I am going to remember that Jesus is in the boat with me. And He will either calm the storm I'm in or calm the storm in me.

Whatever you are going through today, know this: Jesus is right there with you. He can calm the storm you're in and calm the storm in you.

Let's Pray

Dear heavenly Father, thank You for never leaving me. I know that no matter what happens in my life today, You are with me, Your power is in me, and Your protection surrounds me. I have nothing to fear. In Jesus's name, amen.

6

Now It's Your Turn

- On a scale of one to ten, how would you rate your God-trusting level on a daily basis?
- What area(s) of your life do you find to be the most difficult to trust God with?
- What specific ways and circumstances do you need to trust God with right now?
- What friend has stood by you through hard times in the past? How has that made you feel? Are you that trustworthy girlfriend to anyone else?
- Have you gone through a trial where you knew without a doubt that God was with you in and through it? Share a story with your coffee GiG, your GiG group, on the "Trusting God" page of our GiG website (www.GirlfriendsInGod.com/ TrustingGod), or on our Facebook page (www.Facebook.com/ GirlfriendsInGod).
- God's Word promises again and again that His presence in our lives is constant and that He will never leave or forsake us. Read Isaiah 43:2:

When you pass through the waters,
  I will be with you;
and when you pass through the rivers,
  they will not sweep over you.
When you walk through the fire,
  you will not be burned;
  the flames will not set you ablaze.

> How can remembering these truths affect your ability and/or willingness to trust God?

- What experiences or people—positive or negative—has God used in your life to melt away some of the impurities? How? What lessons have you learned?
- Do you really believe that God loves you, or do you resist the bigness of that reality? How does it affect your faith? Be honest.
- Read Psalm 40:1–3: "I waited patiently for the LORD; he turned to me and heard my cry. He lifted me out of the slimy pit, out of the mud and mire; he set my feet on a rock and gave me a firm place to stand. He put a new song in my mouth, a hymn of praise to our God. Many will see and fear the LORD and put their trust in him."

> Discuss or journal about what this psalm means to you personally.

- Wrap up your response time with prayer. Move from confession, to adoration, to thanksgiving, and end with your petitions (personal prayer needs).

Your GiG Trust Adventure Journal

Spend a few moments contemplating and journaling about some of the scriptural truths that moved your heart as you read the devotions this week. Then write a prayer of response to God.

_____
_____
_____
_____
_____
_____
_____
_____
_____
_____
_____
_____
_____
_____
_____
_____
_____
_____

Do not be afraid. Stand firm and you will see the deliverance the LORD will bring you today.... The LORD will fight for you; you need only to be still. (Exodus 14:13–14)

1

Soul Blinders

Gwen Smith

Today's Truth

So be careful to do what the LORD your God has commanded you; do not turn aside to the right or to the left. (Deuteronomy 5:32)

Friend to Friend

When I was a young girl, I rode horses with my cousin Beth. When she was prepping her horse for shows, Beth would often add blinders to the horse's bridle. Horse trainers believe these blinders, also called blinkers or winkers, keep the horse focused on what is in front of it and encourage it to pay attention to the show rather than to other distractions, such as crowds. Now, I'm not a horse, but at times the eyes of my heart do wander, and I get distracted from what really matters. It makes me think that I could benefit from some "soul blinders."

You see, I have this distraction problem. At times I look around at what others are doing, being, and accomplishing and feel ineffective, unproductive, and unnecessary. When I'm distracted, it becomes harder for me to trust God. There. I said it. It's not pretty, but it's true.

When do I have this problem? Whenever I look around instead of looking to God. (How bizarre! I even know the answer to my problem...and I still struggle with it!) Do you ever do that? Do you compare yourself to others and, as a result, determine that there are great deficiencies in your life? Do you ever feel like you don't measure up to those around you? Join the club. I bet we all struggle with this at times.

The good news is that God doesn't leave us without direction or help. He gave us His Word, the Bible, to direct our thoughts, behaviors, hearts, minds, and souls—to be our soul blinders! Scripture reminds us of this in Deuteronomy 5:32–33.

> So be careful to do what the LORD your God has commanded you; do not turn aside to the right or to the left.
> Walk in obedience to all that the LORD your God has commanded you, so that you may live and prosper and prolong your days in the land that you will possess.

God inspired King Solomon to say it this way:

> Keep my commands and you will live;
>   guard my teachings as the apple of your eye.
> Bind them on your fingers;
>   write them on the tablet of your heart.
> Say to wisdom, "You are my sister,"
>   and to insight, "You are my relative." (Proverbs 7:2–4)

Ahhh...and the light bulbs turn on! When we look to the Lord—to His plan that is unique to each of us—we will prosper. And when we look to the right and to the left, we lose our focus, we

worry about comparison, we become distracted, and we fail to trust God and His Word. So, like Paul, let's press on. Forward. With a gaze committed to the path ahead, not to the path that is behind us or on either side. Sister, as the apostle Paul said,

> I do not consider myself yet to have taken hold of it. But one thing I do: Forgetting what is behind and straining toward what is ahead, I press on toward the goal to win the prize for which God has called me heavenward in Christ Jesus. (Philippians 3:13–14)

Today, I pray that you will join me in asking God to give us soul blinders, because when we turn our eyes upon Jesus and look full in His wonderful face, the things of earth—the distractions, the comparisons, and the stuff that causes us to lose our focus—will grow strangely dim in the light of His glory and grace. Our faith and trust in God will blind us from all these earthly concerns.

Let's Pray

Dear God, thanks for giving us the Bible to direct us in life. I ask that You would put blinders on the eyes of my heart so that I will be solely focused on living for You. I pray as the psalmist does: "I gain understanding from your precepts; therefore I hate every wrong path. Your word is a lamp for my feet, a light on my path. I have taken an oath and confirmed it, that I will follow your righteous laws" (Psalm 119:104–106). Please help me to fully trust in You and follow Your ways. In Jesus's name I pray, amen.

Stop! Drop! Roll!

Mary Southerland

Today's Truth

This I declare about the LORD: He alone is my refuge, my place of safety; he is my God, and I trust him. (Psalm 91:2, NLT)

Friend to Friend

A friend recently e-mailed me the following message with a subject line that read, "I immediately thought of you when I read this!"

"Life should not be a journey to the grave with the intention of arriving safely in a pretty and well-preserved body. But rather to skid in broadside, thoroughly used up, totally worn out and loudly proclaiming, 'Wow, what a ride!'"

As I read the words on the computer screen, I wasn't sure if I had just received a sweet compliment or some badly needed correction—or both. The part about arriving at the grave in a pretty and well-preserved body was flattering, but the part about being thoroughly used up and totally worn out—well, not so much. My next thought was, "Boredom is highly underrated!" I suspect that the truth lies somewhere in between, maybe around the area of balance.

"Contrary to popular belief and the way that I have lived a great

deal of my life, balance is not a dirty word. In fact, a balanced life is a powerful life. It must be." I wrote those exact words in one of my books. I also stated that a busy life is not necessarily a productive life. I think it is time for a refresher course on how to find God's balance in life because being out of balance is not a good thing. When our finances are out of balance, we hear from the bank. When the washer is out of balance, it dances across the floor. When the tires on our car are out of balance, the ride is rough. But when our life is out of balance, disaster is just around the corner.

As I was praying about this devotional, the Father brought to mind my elementary school days when the firemen came to our school to teach us what we should do in case we ever caught on fire. I remember the drill clearly: Stop! Drop! Roll! Let's apply that same drill to the area of balance.

Stop! When was the last time you stopped, got off the merry-go-round, and moved out of the fast lane to take a long, hard look at your life? It is so easy to live each day just doing "the next thing" that comes along. The one-size-fits-all mentality about life plans is from the pit and smells like smoke, girlfriend. God has a plan for your life that is unique, and you are the only person who can be "you." Build on your strengths. Accept your limitations and yield to the seasons of life. Get in the Word and ask God to show you His plan.

Drop! Once you discover your life plan, eliminate anything that does not fit that plan. Learn to invest your time instead of just spending it or allowing others to steal it. We are all responsible for how we spend the time God has given us. Every morning we are credited with 86,400 seconds. No balance is carried into the next day and every night erases what we fail to use. Choose to budget your time just as you budget your money and learn to say no without feeling guilty.

Roll! Roll away the burdens you are carrying, and learn the value of resting in God. Every opportunity to worry is also an opportunity to trust Him. I heard a story about a man who had to cross a wide, frozen river. He was afraid the ice might be too thin, so he began to crawl on his hands and knees in fear, thinking he would fall through the icy surface at any time. Just as he neared the opposite shore, exhausted and weak, another man glided past him sitting on a sled loaded with iron. Like that ice, the promises of God will not break under the weight of any problem or trial you will ever face. Take Him at His Word. Let God be God in your life, and trust Him.

You may have already mastered the spiritual discipline of a balanced life. If so, all I can say is "You go, girl!" But if you are waiting for your life to fall into place, hoping that the things you are doing will achieve the balance you long for, I encourage you to stop, drop, and roll!

Let's Pray

Father, I am tired. My life is out of control and I don't know what to do. Please help me examine my priorities by Your standards and expectations and to live for Your pleasure and glory. I choose now to trust You, knowing that You are in control whether it looks like it or not. My faith is weak, Lord. Strengthen me to do what You created me to do. In Jesus's name, amen.

I Need Rest!

Gwen Smith

Today's Truth

The apostles gathered around Jesus and reported to him all they had done and taught. Then, because so many people were coming and going that they did not even have a chance to eat, he said to them, "Come with me by yourselves to a quiet place and get some rest." So they went away by themselves in a boat to a solitary place. (Mark 6:30–32)

Friend to Friend

I spin plates. Not real plates, but metaphorical plates. I spin lots of plates at the same time, and I multitask. This is both a blessing and a curse in my life. Sometimes I'm energized by the amount of things I can get done in a small window of time…while at other times, my attention is divided in too many directions, leaving me harried. Regardless, there just never seems to be enough hours in the day to get things done or enough hours in the night to give me complete rest.

Being a plate-spinning mom is a challenge. When my kids want me, they don't like to wait for me to spin three more plates before I answer them or give them my attention. But when my daughter

Kennedy was a toddler, she figured out a way to stop me mid-task, no matter what I was doing. She would place her chubby little hands on my cheeks, look me in the eye, and demand my full attention. Then she would deliver her message or question to me. I became her captive audience.

Just as Kennedy used to seek my attention, the Spirit of the Lord often speaks a similar message to my heart: *Don't forget about Me, Gwen! I know you have a lot going on, but your attention should be Mine. I love you. Come sit with Me awhile.*

You and I are busy. Each day we have activities, tasks, and distractions that vie for our time and attention. If we aren't careful and deliberate, our relationship with God can suffer as a result. The Lord doesn't want to be an afterthought, and He doesn't want to be merely penciled in to our schedules. He wants us to prioritize Him, to focus our hearts on Him, worship Him, be with Him, rest in Him. The more we know Him, the easier it is to trust Him. What are your priorities? Where does God fit into your schedule? How vital is it to you that you spend one-on-one time with God each day? Are you experiencing the supernatural rest that's found in His presence?

In Mark 6:30–32, we learn that Jesus and His apostles had been busy working for their heavenly Father. In fact, they had worked with such vigor that they hadn't even gotten a decent meal in their bellies. (Boy, do I know what that's like!) In response, Jesus invited them to get away with Him so they could find some rest and rejuvenation in His presence. He said, "Come with me by yourselves to a quiet place and get some rest" (Mark 6:31). That same invitation is extended to you and me.

God wants you to pause the plate spinning and be His captive audience in this very moment. He wants you to go with Him to a quiet place: to be still, to gaze into His eyes, to worship Him in Spirit

and in truth, to be lost in His glory and found by His grace—to find rest. Trust is found in the resting, in the dwelling with Him.

I'd like you to imagine His strong yet gentle hands reaching for your cheeks, lifting your chin, and drawing your eyes to His. Fix your gaze on His beautiful, blazing, mercy-filled eyes. Give the Lord your full attention. He will be your rest.

Let's Pray

Heavenly Father, please forgive me for all the times I fail to give You my attention. I shake my head in wonder at the very thought that You want to lock gazes with someone like me, yet Scripture clearly tells me that You desire to be sought after and found by me. I'm here, Lord. You have my full attention; please speak to my heart and help me be Your captive audience throughout today and every day. In Jesus's name, amen.

Surprise! Surprise!

Sharon Jaynes

Today's Truth

He is the Rock, his works are perfect, and all his ways are just. (Deuteronomy 32:4)

Friend to Friend

When I was eight years old, my prized possession was a collie dog named—what else?—Lassie. She was my shadow. Lassie ran alongside me as I pedaled around the neighborhood on my pink-glittered banana-seat bike. She slept outside the door of my one-room playhouse when my best friend, Wanda, and I "camped out." She protected me from dangerous strangers like the paperboy, the mailman, and the trash collector.

When the veterinarian told us that Lassie had an incurable skin disease and needed to be put to sleep, I was devastated. And even though she was my dog, my dad was almost as heartbroken as I was. He could not bring himself to purposely end Lassie's life, so he drove her out to an old farmhouse about fifteen miles from town.

"Could you please take care of my dog for me?" he asked the old farmer. "She's got a skin disease, but I can't bring myself to put her down."

"Sure," the fellow agreed. "Just leave her here. We'll look after her for you."

I never did get the particulars. Did my dad pay the man? Was he a nice man? Did he have children? All I knew was that Dad had done the best he could.

Months later, Dad went by to check in on the old girl. "I'm sorry, Mr. Edwards," the old farmer said. "Lassie ran away a few days after you left her here. We've never seen her since."

Dad never told me Lassie had run away. But each time he drove into Tarboro, the town near where he had left her, he panned the landscape, looking for a lost dog that answered to the name of Lassie. Miraculously, one day he spotted a collie wandering around the street. Dad jumped out of the car, pulled his pipe out of his mouth, and called out, "Lassie! Here, girl! Come here, girl!" As he clapped his hands together, the dog bounded toward my dad, almost knocking him off his feet. A flurry of fur, tail wagging, and sloppy dog kisses smothered Dad as the two were reunited. What a surprise we had that evening when Lassie came cruising home in the gray Buick.

"Lassie! Lassie!" I cried.

I had never seen such a welcome sight. As a matter of fact, her skin disease was completely gone, and her coat was thicker and more beautiful than ever. All was well with the world.

Two weeks later my older brother was out in the yard wrestling with Lassie. Dazed and ashen faced, he stumbled through the door.

"Mom, we've got a big problem," he said. "You know Lassie? Well…well…she's not a lassie at all. She's a laddie. This dog is a boy!"

"What!" my mother exclaimed.

We ran outside and rolled Lassie (Laddie) over on her (his) back and discovered the truth: *she* was a *he*—and this was not our dog! No wonder her (his) coat looked so thick and healthy.

"Mom," I said, "if this isn't Lassie, then who is it? We've stolen someone's dog!"

Needless to say, we put ads in the Tarboro and Rocky Mount papers, but no one ever claimed Laddie. He seemed perfectly content at our home, so there he stayed.

Have you ever wanted something so badly—hunted, searched, and maybe even prayed for it—but then, when you found it, you realized that maybe it wasn't exactly what you wanted, but it was definitely what you needed? I wanted my dog back. Laddie wanted a family. And for one little girl and a stray pup, God answered my prayer. As usual, His answer had an unexpected twist, but it was perfect in every way.

All through the Bible we see God answering prayer in unexpected ways. The Israelite slaves in Egypt prayed for deliverance, and God sent them a stuttering old man named Moses. Samuel prayed for a new king, and God directed him to Jesse's house to anoint a teenage boy named David. The Hebrew nation prayed for a Savior, and God answered them with a baby's cry in a Bethlehem stable. Surprises all.

Today, as you are lifting up your requests to God, can you trust Him to answer your prayers in His own timing and in His own way? If so, you might experience some unexpected twists and turns that are perfect in every way.

Let's Pray

Dear heavenly Father, I know that Your ways are so much higher than my ways. Today, I trust You to fulfill my deepest longings in Your perfect time and in Your perfect way. Please keep me from interfering with Your plans and trying to make my requests come to fruition on my own. I am waiting for Your surprises. In Jesus's name, amen.

Learning to Breathe

Gwen Smith

Today's Truth

Discipline yourself for the purpose of godliness. (1 Timothy 4:7, NASB)

Friend to Friend

Before our first child was born, my husband and I took a series of classes to prepare us for childbirth. I vividly remember being told by my Lamaze instructor that, while in labor, I would need to breathe through each contraction. She would give us instructions like, "Breathe in through your nose, out through your mouth," and "When you inhale, allow your belly to expand first, then your chest." She told us that the way we breathe would affect the way we would experience labor.

We spent a lot of time during those week-after-week classes learning how to breathe in a whole new way. We were taught that the breaths we would take during labor would need to be purposed and controlled. They required discipline and were not like natural breathing. So I practiced and I practiced the special breathing techniques in preparation for when the labor pains came a-knocking.

When the day arrived to welcome my firstborn son, Preston

Miles Smith, into the world, I learned what a discipline breathing through contractions really is! There were times during labor when I felt like holding my breath instead of breathing. Times when the pain was so intense that my natural response was to scream instead of to breathe. Yes, this type of breathing was surely a learned behavior, a purposed discipline. And on the other side of this purposed discipline, in spite of all the pain endured, I was blessed to experience the wonderful joy of new life.

I've labored through many hard life experiences since my child-birthing days. I'm sure you have too. There are times when circumstances press us in waves, contractions of life that are seemingly endless. When the waves of trials hit our hearts and homes, the spiritual discipline of trusting God helps us to breathe through the squeeze of each pressure. I like to call it faith-breathing. When we hunker down and put into practice the act—the discipline—of faith.

But what do we mean by "the discipline of faith"? Paul wrote:

> Do you not know that in a race all the runners run, but only
> one gets the prize? Run in such a way as to get the prize.
> Everyone who competes in the games goes into strict training.
> They do it to get a crown that will not last, but we do it to get
> a crown that will last forever. (1 Corinthians 9:24–25)

Just as I learned to breathe in preparation for going through labor pains, Christians learn to breathe through life pains when we implement spiritual disciplines in our lives like prayer, fasting, journaling, and Scripture reading. They are purposed disciplines that allow us to experience joy, strength, and eternal perspective in the midst of hard times. The more we pray, the more we grow in inti-

macy with God. The more we read and know the Bible, the more we understand God's will and character. We see over and over again that He is good, faithful, compassionate, loving, gentle, just, holy, righteous, and trustworthy in all things. We are encouraged and spurred on by the faith of others. We learn to faith-breathe!

God is always with us and will help us breathe through the difficult situations we face. He allows us to go through trials as a part of our refining process. Struggles send us running to God for help, for faith, for strength, for protection, and for direction. They are often pregnant with pain, bursting with heartache. If we yield them to God, He uses them to rid our lives of trust barriers like fear and doubt and to bring glory and honor to Him.

There are many life contractions that hurt us, but there is no earthly pain that can diminish the hope of our salvation. We must simply breathe—continue practicing those spiritual disciplines that bind us to the heart of God.

> Yes, and everyone who wants to live a godly life in Christ
> Jesus will suffer persecution…. But you must remain faithful
> to the things you have been taught. You know they are true,
> for you know you can trust those who taught you. You have
> been taught the holy Scriptures from childhood, and they
> have given you the wisdom to receive the salvation that
> comes by trusting in Christ Jesus. All Scripture is inspired
> by God and is useful to teach us what is true and to make
> us realize what is wrong in our lives. It corrects us when we
> are wrong and teaches us to do what is right. God uses it
> to prepare and equip his people to do every good work.
> (2 Timothy 3:12, 14–17, NLT)

Trusting God takes discipline. We don't always feel like it. It's not always what we want to do. It's not natural. At times we feel overwhelmed and want to soul-scream. If we always acted on our feelings, our lives would be chaotic messes. As in childbirth, there finally comes the time of deliverance where what is birthed forth to joy is directly the result of the very pain we have gone through.

Let's Pray

Dear Father, please teach me to breathe! Strengthen me through life's hard labor experiences and help me to practice the disciplines I have learned through Your Scriptures. When I feel like screaming through the pain, help me to breathe by reading and memorizing Your Word, fasting and praying, and meditating on Your truth. Thank You for the strength You will give me as I trust in You. In Jesus's name I pray, amen.

Now It's Your Turn

- There are many things in life that can wear us out and distract us from trusting God. Name a few of the distractions you have come up against in the past or are experiencing now.

- Balance. This is a tough one, isn't it? To lighten up this heavy topic, let's go hypothetical. If you were Goldilocks and you pulled a chair up to the balance table, which of the following best describes the bowl that you've been sipping from lately?

  A. Too hot! I've got too much going on and I know it! ("Don't *even* get me near a balance scale because I'm pretty sure it would break!")

  B. Too cold! I need to get out more! ("Anyone want to go grab a bite to eat after we finish with these questions?")

  C. Just right! I've learned to set boundaries and eliminate excess, and I am trying each day to let God establish my priorities. ("Pass the chocolate, girlfriend. Life is gettin' good!")

- How does sipping from your current balance bowl affect your ability or willingness to trust God?

- After Jesus's disciples had poured themselves out into other people and were exhausted and hungry, Jesus extended them this beautiful invitation: "Come with me by yourselves to a quiet place and get some rest" (Mark 6:31). Do you think Jesus meant physical rest or soul rest?
- Do you think that this "rest" invitation is open to you each day? If so, what would the benefits look like if you took Jesus up on His invitation?
- Part of resting in God is trusting Him to answer your prayers in His own time and in His own way. Write down or share with your girlfriends a time when God answered a prayer in a totally unexpected way.
- Wrap up your response time with prayer. Move from confession, to adoration, to thanksgiving, and end with your petitions (personal prayer needs).

YOUR GiG TRUST ADVENTURE JOURNAL

Spend a few moments contemplating and journaling about some of the scriptural truths that moved your heart as you read the devotions this week. Then write a prayer of response to God.

_____

_____

_____

_____

_____

_____

_____

_____

_____

_____

_____

_____

_____

_____

_____

_____

_____

_____

_____

_____

This I declare about the LORD: He alone is my refuge, my place of safety; he is my God, and I trust him (Psalm 91:2, NLT).

Failure Is Not Final

Mary Southerland

Today's Truth

And we know that in all things God works for the good of those who love him, who have been called according to his purpose. (Romans 8:28)

Friend to Friend

I have never met a single person whose goal in life was to fail, but failure is a reality of life. The key to success is not avoiding failure; it is learning how to handle failure.

- Beethoven's music teacher said he was a hopeless composer.
- Abraham Lincoln campaigned for a seat in the Illinois General Assembly and failed.
- Walt Disney was fired by the editor of a newspaper for lacking creativity.
- The Ford Motor Company was Henry Ford's third business. The first two didn't work out.
- A teacher told Thomas Edison that he was too stupid to learn anything.
- Babe Ruth struck out 1,330 times.

I remember the first time I failed a test. I was in elementary school and my teacher, Mrs. Martin, decided to test us on the names of the states and their capitals. We had been studying them for what seemed like an eternity. I did *not* like geography, so I tended to daydream my way through class. Why did I need to know the names of states I would probably never visit? And what was the big deal about state capitals? As far as I could tell from the pictures in my geography book, the cities all looked pretty much the same to me—boring.

Even though I didn't like geography, I had to make 100 on the test. Why? Because although I was only a child, I knew the unspoken rule that failing a test meant I was a failure.

When Mrs. Martin told us to clear our desks except for one pencil, I panicked. A quick glance at the assignment board revealed nothing. The look of confusion on the faces of my classmates told me that they were just as clueless as I was.

"We are having a little test to see how you are doing in geography," Mrs. Martin explained. I had three problems with her statement. First, there is no such thing as a "little" test. Second, no one had said anything about having a test. And third, I did not know the names of the states and their capitals. When I voiced my complaints, Mrs. Martin smiled and said it was a pop quiz.

Side note: That might have been the moment when I decided to become an elementary school teacher but vowed to never subject my students to the terror of pop quizzes.

My stomach dropped, and I broke out in a cold sweat. My mind raced as I frantically searched for my geography book. Maybe I could learn the names of a capital or two while she handed out the tests. "No books allowed," Mrs. Martin warned. I was doomed.

When the blank outline of the United States appeared on my

desk, I burst into tears. Mrs. Martin asked the student teacher to take over as she gently ushered me out of the classroom and into the nurse's office next door.

When I finally stopped crying, Mrs. Martin said, "Honey, what's wrong?"

I could not believe my ears. "I don't know the names of the states or their capitals," I wailed out what seemed to be a ridiculously obvious explanation.

"Do you know some of them?" she asked.

I thought for a moment. "I know *some* of them but not all of them, and that means I'll fail the test," I responded.

"Why don't you just do your best and see what happens?" she suggested. I did my best…and I still failed the test.

Guess what? The world kept spinning. I passed elementary school with flying colors, graduated from high school with honors, attended college on a music and academic scholarship, and eventually became an elementary teacher. And I failed a lot along the way. So did a lot of people in the Bible.

Adam and Eve blatantly disobeyed God and then lied about their sin. David committed adultery with Bathsheba and then plotted the murder of her husband. Peter bragged about his commitment to Jesus and then denied Him not once, but three times. In fact, it's hard to find biblical characters who didn't fail at some point, but those who learned from their failure and used it as a tool of growth were often used by God to accomplish great things.

I have come to believe that failure is a necessary part of our growth and maturity as followers of Jesus Christ. Failure can interpret the unconditional love and forgiveness of God like nothing else can—if we trust God enough to transform tragedy into triumph.

Desperation can be our friend if it makes us crave God and long to see His power unleashed in our lives. Failure is not final, but God's grace is.

Let's Pray

Father, I know that I have failed You. Forgive me for the sin in my life. Thank You for Your love and mercy that covers that sin. Help me learn the lesson that each failure holds. Teach me to trust You with my whole life—failures and all. In Jesus's name, amen.

Gone with the Wind

Sharon Jaynes

Today's Truth

When Moses was forty years old, he decided to visit his own people, the Israelites.... After forty years [more] had passed, an angel appeared to Moses in the flames of a burning bush in the desert near Mount Sinai. (Acts 7:23, 30)

Friend to Friend

"As God is my witness, I will never be hungry again!" I bet you know what movie that line came from. But at sixteen, my son had no idea.

Several years ago, the epic drama *Gone with the Wind* was re-released in theaters all across America. This digitally enhanced, chromatically improved icon took us back to a time in history when America was experiencing a paradigm shift. My husband and I thought it would be important for our teenage son to have the *Gone with the Wind* experience on the big screen, so we purchased three tickets and settled in for what we knew would be a long evening. We watched as the plantation owners of the Old South held grand parties, and Scarlett O'Hara batted her eyelashes at all the men crowded around her tiny feet. Beautiful plantations, bountiful flowers, and

Southern opulence filled the scenes with merriment at every turn. The scenery changed as the Civil War began, Scarlett became a widow (twice), and Rhett tried to save the day.

After about two hours, a sullied Miss Scarlett, who had been deserted by Rhett Butler, stood on a hillside with Atlanta burning in the background. She shook her fist in the air. Sweat poured from her porcelain brow, dirt clung to her tattered hoop skirt, and mud covered her tear-stained face. She shook her fist in the air and adamantly decreed, "As God is my witness, I will never be hungry again!"

Then the curtain fell.

Steven looked at me and said, "That was a strange way to end."

But I pointed his attention back to the screen. *Intermission*. The movie was only halfway over!

"You've got to be kidding," he sighed.

Have you ever felt like Scarlett? Your plans go up in flames, your friends desert you, and you long for the good life? I think the producers of *Gone with the Wind* had the right idea. Maybe we need to take an intermission—take a deep breath, refocus on God, and remember: God's not finished with the movie of our lives yet. Perhaps we're just in an intermission.

Looking back in the Bible, we see many men and women who came to a point in their lives where they thought it was the end, only later to discover it was merely an intermission. Elijah hid in a cave thinking his ministry as a prophet was over, only to be roused by God and told to continue on. Moses herded sheep in the desert believing that his dream to rescue the Hebrews was dashed, until God spoke to him through a burning bush and told him to go to Egypt. The prophet Samuel groveled in depression after King Saul disobeyed God and lost his reign. But then God told Samuel to get up out of bed, put oil in his horn, and travel to Bethlehem to anoint the

new king of Israel. Each of these men thought it was the end, but in reality, it was only an intermission. God wasn't finished with the drama of their lives quite yet.

I don't know what you're facing today. Perhaps your life has taken you to an unexpected place. Perhaps, like Moses, you've made a poor decision that resulted in your running from God and from man. Perhaps, like Elijah, you've allowed someone's threats to put fear in your heart and you're in hiding. Perhaps, like Samuel, you're depressed because someone you oversee (a child, for example) didn't turn out like you had hoped. Perhaps, as your dreams burned in the background, you've stood on the hillside with fist raised in the air making declarations to God.

If you see yourself on the screen, can I encourage you to stretch, sit down, take a deep breath, and regroup? Your story's not over yet. Perhaps you're just at an intermission. As someone once said, we shouldn't put a period where God put a comma. And if you are in an intermission right now, don't waste the time. Learn to listen to God's voice through His Word, prayer, circumstances, nature, and His people…and get ready. The curtain is about to rise.

Let's Pray

Heavenly Father, help me not to put a period where You put a comma. Thank You for being the director of the grand drama of my life. Help me not to waste time during the intermissions of my life, but to use the quiet days to become a woman who listens to You. And when the time comes and the curtain rises on a new phase of my life, help me to be ready to do whatever You have planned for me to do. In Jesus's name, amen.

Yes and Amen!

Gwen Smith

Today's Truth

For no matter how many promises God has made, they are "Yes" in Christ. And so through him the "Amen" is spoken by us to the glory of God. (2 Corinthians 1:20)

Friend to Friend

When my son, Preston, was in sixth grade, he chose to plant spinach for his science fair project. He planted seeds in four plastic cups and watered each batch with a fixed daily amount of four different liquids: water, orange juice, cola, and milk. (Yes, you are correct! By day three of his fourteen-day project, the milk cup reeked to high heavens with a stinky-sour smell!) Preston's hypothesis was that the seeds watered with water would grow faster than the seeds watered with orange juice, cola, and milk.

Once his hypothesis was determined, Preston and I (his faithful mommy/research assistant) diligently went about the task of collecting data, watering the seeds, taking pictures, and documenting his findings. The instructions on the back of the seed envelope indicated

that we should see spinach sprouts within seven to ten days. Preston was looking forward to seeing the sprouts and was eager to see if his hypothesis was valid. I was too.

So we watered and we waited. We stayed the course and did the work required with hearts that were eager to witness a green, leafy harvest. Day seven came and went. No sprouts. Day eight came and went. No sprouts. Day nine. No sprouts. Day ten. No sprouts.

When all was said and done, we were disappointed that Preston's faithful efforts did not bear spinach. In fourteen days not one green sprout shot up from any of the cups. In fact, we saw no evidence of any growth at all—not even on a root level. And although his data got collected, his project got completed, and Preston received a good grade, we were both heart-sad that we didn't get to see any growth.

Sometimes our lives are like that science fair project. We invest in others and wait eagerly to see the harvest. We obey God, trust His plan, and walk according to His Word. We plant seeds into the soil of our marriages or dating relationships and water them with love, hope, service, and truth. We plant seeds into the life-soil of our friends and coworkers and water them with loyalty, time, and encouragement. As parents and grandparents we "grow" our children and our grandchildren. We water them with love and feed them with the Word. We water and we wait with great expectations in our hearts and a desire to see some growth. We long to see the fruit of our labor.

At times we see fruit.

At times we don't.

Jesus gave His disciples a trustworthy promise that if we stick to His side and stay tight to God's will, our lives and our efforts *will* bear fruit. He made this promise:

Remain in me, as I also remain in you. No branch can bear
fruit by itself; it must remain in the vine. Neither can you
bear fruit unless you remain in me.

I am the vine; you are the branches. If you remain in me
and I in you, you will bear much fruit; apart from me you
can do nothing. (John 15:4–5)

When we remain in Jesus—when we trust God by turning to
the Holy Spirit for guidance and to His Word for truth—you and I
will bear fruit, whether we see it or not.

A person of faith believes God's promises because His promises
are connected to His character. God's promises aren't flippant.
They're secure! The apostle Paul said it like this:

Whatever God has promised gets stamped with the Yes of
Jesus. In him, this is what we preach and pray, the great
Amen, God's Yes and our Yes together, gloriously evident.
God affirms us, making us a sure thing in Christ, putting
his Yes within us. By his Spirit he has stamped us with his
eternal pledge—a sure beginning of what he is destined to
complete. (2 Corinthians 1:20–22, MSG).

You see, friend, the yes-and-amen promise here is that we will
bear fruit, not that we will necessarily *see* the fruit in our own timing
or even in our own lifetimes. Understanding this promise sure does
help me to trust God more. And further, knowing that our faithfulness will directly impact how much fruit will be produced should
challenge us to remain faithful!

All of the promises of our covenant God are "yes" and "amen."
We can trust His Word to be true because the character of our God

is unblemished. Apart from Him, we can do nothing. When we remain in Him, we will bear fruit. Sometimes we will see it. Sometimes we won't.

Our God-confidence is bolstered when we remember that He is faithful, and that our job is to listen, seek, and obey—to remain in Him—not to try to control the outcome of the seeds that He instructs us to sow. When we grow in our understanding of God's character and rest in the knowledge that He is for us, not against us (see Romans 8:31), this helps us to trust Him. Let's strive to be women who take God at His Word and believe His "yes" and "amen" promises!

Let's Pray

Dear Lord, thank You for planting a seed of faith in the soil of my heart through Your Son, Jesus Christ. Please grow my faith. Help me to trust You more and remind me to fix my eyes on You, not on the results of my life investments. In Jesus's name I pray, amen.

When I Fall Down

Mary Southerland

Today's Truth

Whoever dwells in the shelter of the Most High will rest in the shadow of the Almighty. I will say of the LORD, "He is my refuge and my fortress, my God, in whom I trust." (Psalm 91:1–2)

Friend to Friend

I had forgotten just how amazing the process of learning to walk really is until our youngest grandchild reminded me. Justus was a speed crawler who could scoot along the floor almost as fast as I could walk, and he seemed content to explore the bottom of tables and chairs, play with doorstops, or inspect flecks of lint, food crumbs, and the floor at close range. For the first twelve months of his life, that was enough.

However, the day came when Justus was no longer satisfied with exploring his world from the vantage point of his two little hands and knees, and he began pulling himself up on various pieces of furniture. Evidently he liked what he saw because he soon grew tired of just being upright and quickly graduated to the "one step" method of walking.

Throughout the day, Justus carefully and repeatedly pulled himself up on the living room sofa. The toddler shuffle came next as Justus tentatively positioned his stout and very determined little thirteen-month-old body between the sofa and loveseat. Pausing to catch his breath and gather his courage, Justus stared longingly at his goal, the armrest of the loveseat. His big brown eyes seemed to measure the size of the step he would have to take in order to reach his final destination and thus master that long-held toddler tradition of cruising the furniture.

Eventually, he would let go of the sofa cushion, take "one step," and quickly grab hold of the loveseat. Most of the time this brave little man then looked over his shoulder at whoever happened to be watching, a huge grin lighting up his face and the entire room. That was the cue for applause. And believe me, we always applauded. Yes, the "one step" method of walking served Justus well—until he decided that what he wanted was not anywhere near the sofa or loveseat—and a new strategy was required.

I can imagine his little heart beating with excitement and fear as he realized the profound ramifications of his next move. He had to completely let go of that sofa and loveseat and walk where he had never been—into thin air—with no safety net.

And then it happened. Justus let go and took a step...then another...and another! We held our breath as we watched this special little boy actually walk for the very first time in his life. When he wobbled and fell to the floor, our daughter instinctively reached out to catch her precious child. He didn't see her at first, but when he looked up...there she was. She had been nearby, watching the whole time. Danna squealed with joy, grabbed Justus in a fierce hug, and twirled him around the room, laughing and yelling, "Good job! You did it! You walked, buddy!"

My husband and I joined in the celebration, clapping and cheering along with our daughter. Justus decided that his accomplishment must be worthy of praise, and he began to clap as well. In fact, he was so excited that he fell to the floor, kicking, laughing, and clapping. It was both hilarious and profound.

Have you ever felt like you have taken the step God wanted you to take only to find yourself dangling in thin air with no safety net in sight? I have. I don't like it. I want to know what is just ahead and see what is around the next corner of life. It frightens me to take risks. I wonder if God will really be there and come through for me the way He says He will in the Bible. Can I really do what God is asking me to do? Will He be pleased by my seemingly insignificant step of faith? And what happens if I fall? Falling is painful and something I try to avoid whenever possible.

I have great news for you, girlfriend! God is near. His eyes are set on you and His heart delights in your very existence as His daughter. If you listen carefully, you just might hear Him applauding that one tiny step of faith you were willing to take as you walked straight through your fear. God is fully aware of where you are and what you need. And when you fall, you can rest assured your Father will be there to hold you in His arms of love and strengthen you for every step of your journey.

Let's Pray

Dear God, I want to see and know You as the loving and caring Father that You are. Thank You for Your faithfulness in my life. I praise You for Your unconditional love that gives me hope when life looks hopeless. Thank You for never leaving me to live in my own strength. Today, I celebrate the truth that I am Your child and that when I fall, You will be there. In Jesus's name, amen.

The Look of Love

Sharon Jaynes

Today's Truth

Do not be afraid; you will not be put to shame.... You will forget the shame of your youth. (Isaiah 54:4)

Friend to Friend

Her invisible cloak of shame was so heavy, it dragged on the ground behind her and weighed her petite shoulders down. Hidden beneath her chocolate eyes and beautiful smile was a secret that bore down on her heart. She tried to blink back tears as we talked.

"Gina, do you want to talk about it?" I asked.

"I'm so ashamed!" she cried. "I want to tell someone, but I'm afraid. I've never told anyone."

I was speaking at a women's retreat, and the women had come forward to nail the pain of their past to the cross. Words filled the cards: *abuse, sexual promiscuity, abortion, abandonment, stealing, infidelity, emotional cruelty, incest, rape, lying, cheating.* Women gave their shame to God—what had been done to them and what had been done through them...their own poor decisions.

Everyone left the room, emotionally, spiritually, and physically

free for the first time in many years. Everyone except Gina. We settled in two rocking chairs overlooking the Smoky Mountains, and the fog in Gina's heart began to clear. For the next hour or so, Gina poured out her story of fleeing the advances of her stepfather, living on the street, and engaging in prostitution at the urging of a woman who said she cared.

"I didn't know what to do. I knew I had to get away from my mother's new husband, but I was only seventeen. I didn't have any money. Then I met this woman who seemed to care. She told me there was a way I could make money quick. The first time I did it, I got sick," she cried.

"Every time I did it, a part of me died. I didn't do it for long, but I've never been able to forget the shame and how dirty I felt. Even though I'm now married, have two children, and a wonderful life, I still feel dirty. It was a long time ago, but it feels like yesterday. Nobody knows. My husband doesn't know. He always tells me how precious I am. If he knew, it would kill him."

We talked for a long time about God's forgiveness and the clean slate that He offers us at the cross. Gina knew most of that in her head, but it was her heart that was having trouble believing it could be so easy.

After we talked I asked, "Are you glad you told me?"

"Yes," she said. "Mainly because the way you are looking at me now is not any different from the way that you were looking at me before you knew."

My mind traveled to another incident, one not so different from this precious time with Gina. We don't know her name, but we do know her circumstances. Right in the middle of Jesus's teaching, the Pharisees dragged in a half-dressed woman and threw her at Jesus's feet.

"Teacher, this woman was caught in the act of adultery," they hissed. "The Law of Moses commands us to stone such a woman. Now what do you say?"

Jesus bent down and wrote in the dirt. The silence was deafening as the crowd waited for His response. The Pharisees thought they had finally caught Him between a rock and hard place, and their hearts were as hard as the stones they held in their hands.

What they didn't realize is that there is no hard place for Jesus. Finally, Jesus stood erect, looked each man in the eye, and said, "Let him who is without sin throw the first stone."

One by one the men began to leave. The older ones with the longer list of sins departed first, followed by the younger. When no one was left but Jesus and the accused, He looked at her with compassion and asked, "Woman, where are they? Has no one condemned you?"

"No one, sir," she whispered.

"Then neither do I condemn you," Jesus declared. "Go now and leave your life of sin" (see John 8).

And that's the truth of grace. God's grace—unmerited favor from God, receiving a gift we do not deserve. Whether it is Gina who left a life of prostitution, this unnamed woman caught in adultery, or me and you in our own particular sin, Jesus looks at us with compassion, wipes our slates clean, and whispers, "Then neither do I condemn you. Go and leave your life of sin."

No matter what you've gone through or what mistakes you have made in your life, you can trust Jesus with your deepest pain and darkest secrets. He promises to mend your broken heart and wipe away your shame.

Is there someone you need to extend grace to today? Would you consider yourself a safe place for the hurting to come? Do you hear God extending His grace to you?

Let's Pray

Dear Lord, when others look at me, I pray they see Your grace and mercy in my eyes. Help me to always be a safe place where others can pour out their hearts without fear of condemnation or rejection. You have certainly been that safe place for me. In Jesus's name, amen.

Now It's Your Turn

TIME FOR REFLECTION

- This week we talked about trusting God with our failures, falls, and frustrations. What comes to your mind or heart when you hear the old saying, "We shouldn't put a period where God put a comma"?

- Is there a place in your life where you have put a period and perhaps God has only put a comma? Think about it. Is there something you have given up on? A dream? A person? A calling? Suppose the curtain fell for an intermission and not the end. Did you leave too soon?

- Read Job 14:7: "At least there is hope for a tree: If it is cut down, it will sprout again, and its new shoots will not fail."

  How can you apply this verse to the failures in your life?

- Read Psalm 91:1–2: "Whoever dwells in the shelter of the Most High will rest in the shadow of the Almighty. I will say of the LORD, 'He is my refuge and my fortress, my God, in whom I trust.'"

  Look at the action words in these two verses. What would those actions mean or look like in the life of a person who chooses to trust God even when times are hard? For example:

Action word: *dwells*.

Means: *If I stay under the protection of God (Most High), I will find rest and a shelter from the storms I face in life.*

- When we fail and confess our sin, God offers grace to each of us through His Son, Jesus Christ. Grace is God's unmerited favor toward us, forgiveness we don't deserve. Simple, yet complex. Which of the following statements best represents the way you handle grace?

    A. I'm just not that into grace...because I honestly don't think God's really all that into me. ("What's grace got to do with it?")

    B. I like the concept of grace, but I struggle with applying it to my life and in my relationships. ("I would like someone to give me a connect-the-dots page for grace, please! I seriously find it hard to grasp.")

    C. I like to extend grace more than I am willing to receive grace from God or others. ("I pretty much beat myself up when I make mistakes because I think I deserve the punishment. Freedom is for other people.")

    D. I like to receive grace from God and others more than I am willing to extend it to others. ("I like to be forgiven and free. Now if everyone around me could just get their acts together, I might be more willing to extend grace!")

    E. I'm a total grace girl! ("Bring on the grace. Extra scoop please! Grace for you...grace for me. While we're at it, let's throw in some dark chocolate and some fresh-roasted coffee because a freedom party is about to go down. Thank You, Jesus!")

- Wrap up your response time with prayer. Move from confession, to adoration, to thanksgiving, and end with your petitions (personal prayer needs).

YOUR GIG TRUST ADVENTURE JOURNAL

Spend a few moments contemplating and journaling about some of the scriptural truths that moved your heart as you read the devotions this week. Then write a prayer of response to God.

_____

_____

_____

_____

_____

_____

_____

_____

_____

_____

_____

Finally, brothers and sisters, whatever is true, whatever is noble, whatever is right, whatever is pure, whatever is lovely, whatever is admirable—if anything is excellent or praiseworthy—think about such things. Whatever you have learned or received or heard from me, or seen in me—put it into practice. And the God of peace will be with you (Philippians 4:8–9).

A Fresh-Brewed Faith

Gwen Smith

Today's Truth

Faith comes from hearing, and hearing through the word of Christ.
(Romans 10:17, ESV)

Friend to Friend

Every morning I walk straight to the coffeepot and push the On button. I'm a total coffee girl. I like a piping-hot, extra dark roast with half-and-half, and I struggle to function before my first cup of coffee. I crave that first sip and relish the warmth of the mug in my hands. I jokingly call it my "warm, happy friend." My mornings just wouldn't be the same without coffee!

We should have the same attitude about our faith. We should wake up each morning bursting at the seams to be with God, to be in His presence, to listen for His still small voice, to savor Him. A faith that is brewed fresh daily strengthens us, renews us, and enables us to mount up with wings like eagles, to experience the power of God in our lives, to run and not grow weary, to walk and not faint (see Isaiah 40:29–31).

This energizing, percolated faith is readily available to all who ask, seek, and knock (see Matthew 7:7–8). How can you experience this power in your life? By getting alone with God, reading the Bible, and listening for His voice each day. "Faith comes from hearing, and hearing through the word of Christ" (Romans 10:17, ESV).

Like a morning with no coffee, there are times when we are sluggish in our faith. Times when trusting God doesn't come easily. Times when we need a shot of God-caffeine in our day. A spiritual espresso. What can we do at these times? Are there things in the Scriptures that tell us how we can strengthen our trust-muscles and jump-start our faith? Absolutely!

One practical way to build your faith is by remembrance. When David was just a shepherd boy, he had courage to face a giant partly because he remembered the previous victories the Lord had allowed him to experience. He approached King Saul with great confidence, saying: "The LORD who rescued me from the paw of the lion and the paw of the bear will rescue me from the hand of this Philistine" (1 Samuel 17:37).

David's past victories fueled his faith and helped him to trust God for his present deliverances. Ours do the same. We can face our giants with equal confidence when we pause to remember how the Lord has worked in our past. As Corrie ten Boom put it, "Faith sees the invisible, believes the unbelievable, and receives the impossible."

What has God brought you through in the past? Think on these things, and choose to trust Him to bring you through all you face today and tomorrow. When you trust God with a fresh-brewed faith, He will be your Strength, your Sustainer, and your Hiding Place so you can run and not grow weary, walk and not be faint. Fill up your faith cup right now.

Let's Pray

Dear God, You have brought me through so many challenging times. Please remind me of Your faithfulness in the past so that I may have a fresh shot of faith that equips me to live today in Your strength. Help me to trust You, and keep me from leaning on my own understanding. In Jesus's name, amen.

2

Step Away from the Shore

Mary Southerland

Today's Truth

Between three and six o'clock in the morning, Jesus came to them, walking on the water. (Matthew 14:25, NCV)

Friend to Friend

Faith is the ability to trust what we cannot see. Twentieth-century writer John A. Shedd said, "A ship in harbor is safe—but that is not what ships are built for." Faith is willing to take risks, embrace the unseen, and step away from the safety of the shore. We often fear the outcome or don't understand the step God has asked us to take, so we hesitate. We are afraid to fail and are more concerned about our reputation as a Christian than we are about being obedient to God. As long as the Enemy can keep us preoccupied with a selfish perspective, our faith is impotent.

Authentic faith naturally produces action, but faith is hindered unless we abandon ourselves to that faith. Did you know that the African impala can jump to a height of over ten feet and cover a

distance of greater than thirty feet? Yet these magnificent creatures can be kept in any zoo by a three-foot wall. The animals will not jump if they cannot see where their feet will land.

Many people say they *do* believe God is who He says He is and that He is able to do what He says He will do but falter at the point of believing that God is *willing* to work in their lives. If we don't believe God is willing to keep His promises, we are not walking in faith. Oh, we find it easy to agree mentally with the truth that we serve a powerful God who loves us and has a great plan for our lives, but that belief is worthless until it settles in our hearts and changes the way we live. If we don't live it, we don't really believe it. If we are not willing to step away from the shore, we will miss so much of what God has for us in life.

The story is told of Will Rogers, who went to his friend Eddie Cantor for advice. Will wanted to make some important changes in his act but was worried about the danger of such changes, explaining that he wasn't sure if they would work. Eddie Cantor's response was, "Why not go out on a limb? That's where the fruit is!"

The same is true of faith.

Faith trusts God and believes that God is willing to do what He promises to do. The life of Jesus Christ is the embodiment of God's willingness to work in our lives. The disciples had personally witnessed God's willingness to save His children. Yet, in Matthew 14, we find them in a boat, caught in a storm, afraid, and still questioning God's willingness to rescue them. Did they cry out in fear? Yes! Did He come? Yes!

Jesus went to the disciples, walking on the water, between three and six o'clock in the morning, the darkest time of the night. I have often wished I could have been on that boat with the disciples, waiting for Jesus to show up. I imagine the questions and complaints

were flying. *"Why would Jesus send us out here, knowing the waves were high? Where is He? Why is He waiting so long to rescue us? Can't He just calm the waves like He did before? I ministered all day long and this is my reward? Is He really coming? I don't understand!"* Sound familiar? It does to me.

We are quick to believe the lie that God is angry with us and, as a result, will not bless our lives or meet our needs. The truth is that God is willing and waiting to pour out His favor and blessings on a life of faith. Hebrews tells us that faith always honors God and God always honors faith. "Without faith no one can please God. Anyone who comes to God must believe that he is real and that he rewards those who truly want to find him" (Hebrews 11:6, NCV).

I think part of the problem is that we don't know how to define *blessing*. A blessing is not always easy, painless, simple, comfortable, or expected. A blessing often comes wrapped in the mystery of darkness and pain. But I am learning this truth: anything that makes us cry out to God can be counted as a blessing. Why? Because when we are desperate and hurting, when we have no answers and the darkness is closing in, we cry out to God, just as the disciples did, and He comes. Not because we have earned His presence or His mercy, but because we cried out with a tiny seed of faith, as His children, knowing He is not only able but willing to come. Step away from that shore, girlfriend. He will meet you there.

Let's Pray

Father, I come to You today with a faith that seems so small. I want to believe You, Lord. I want to walk by faith, knowing that You will keep every promise You have ever made. Help my unbelief, Lord. In Jesus's name, amen.

3

The Wreck That Saved Her Life

Sharon Jaynes

Today's Truth

As for God, his way is perfect: The LORD's word is flawless; he shields all who take refuge in him. (2 Samuel 22:31)

Friend to Friend

For five years Gayle had cortisone injections in her painful knee. Because Gayle's mother had joint pain in her knees for most of her adult life, Gayle resigned herself to the same fate—arthritis. The doctors never x-rayed or performed an MRI to diagnose the problem; they merely prescribed treatment according to symptoms and the family history of joint pain.

One night, Gayle, her husband, Joe, and another couple attended a basketball game at their college alma mater. On the way home, Gayle twisted around in her front seat to face the couple in the back. As they chatted, she noticed an 18-wheeler's headlights rapidly approaching their car. *Surely he's going to stop,* she thought. But before

she could even warn the other passengers, the truck plowed into the back of their car at fifty miles per hour. Because of Gayle's position, her knees were smashed into the dashboard.

The driver of the truck had fallen asleep at the wheel and never even applied the brakes before impact. Gayle and Joe's car, a heavy Lincoln Continental, was totaled, but no one in the car was hurt—except Gayle and her arthritic knees, which were black, blue, and swollen within a couple of hours. When Gayle went to the doctor the next day, he decided to take an x-ray to make sure there were no broken bones.

"Gayle," he said, "I don't know how to tell you this, but you have a slow-growing tumor in your right knee."

"A tumor? How long has it been there?" she asked.

"Well, this is a very slow growing type of tumor which has probably been there for several years. The pain that you've been experiencing in the past has most likely been due to the tumor causing the bone to expand as it grows. It wasn't from arthritis after all. We're going to have to remove the tumor right away."

"I can't do it right away," she answered. "I have a two-week counseling course that I'm going to next week. I've been on the waiting list for two years, so this tumor is going to have to wait. You did say it was slow-growing, correct?"

"Yes," he answered, "but I wouldn't wait a day longer than necessary. You are a very lucky young lady. If you had not been in that car accident, we may not have found the tumor until it was too late."

Gayle smiled. Luck had nothing to do with it. She knew God was in control.

Gayle did go to the counseling seminar, where 750 committed Christians gathered around her on the last night and prayed for her knee. The next day, when the doctor went in to remove the tumor,

he was amazed to find that this slow-growing tumor had rapidly begun to shrink.

"Once again," the doctor commented as he showed Gayle the new pre-op x-ray of a much smaller tumor, "you are a lucky girl. The tumor is smaller today than it was two weeks ago."

Once again Gayle knew luck had nothing to do with it. She then shared with the doctor about the 750 people who had prayed for her the night before.

Many times when something seemingly bad happens, we need to remember that God is the director of the grand drama of our lives. We may not understand the whys or the what-fors, but we can trust in the God who controls them all. "Nothing that happens to the child of God is a coincidence, and when we look at every situation and encounter as God-directed, we will more easily fulfill His plan. This knowledge should also make each of us feel needed, valuable, and important: we are fulfilling God's purposes for His Kingdom."[1]

Are there circumstances in your life that you simply don't understand? Have there been twists and turns that have you confused? Rest assured, my friend, God is never surprised or caught off guard. He's in control.

Ponder this poem by A. M. Overton, a Mississippi pastor who penned these words after he lost his wife and baby in childbirth in 1932:

My Father's way may twist and turn,
My heart may throb and ache,
But in my soul I'm glad I know
He maketh no mistake.

1. Kathy Collard Miller, *Women of the Bible* (Lancaster, PA: Starburst, 1999), 149.

My cherished plans may go astray,
My hopes may fade away,
But still I'll trust my Lord to lead
For He does know the way.

Tho' night be dark and it may seem
That day will never break,
I'll pin my faith, my all in Him,
He maketh no mistake.

There's so much now I cannot see,
My eyesight far too dim,
But come what may, I'll simply trust
And leave it all to Him.

For by and by the mist will lift
And plain it all He'll make
Through all the way, tho' dark to me,
He made not one mistake.[2]

Let's Pray

Dear Lord, help me look past my problems to see Your provision and protection. Help me to rest in the truth that Your ways are higher than my ways even when I don't understand. In Jesus's name, amen.

---

2. A. M. Overton, "He Maketh No Mistake" (Baldwyn, MS, 1932, unpublished material), www.churchlead.com/mind_wanderings/view/1630/he_maketh_no_mistake.

A Desperate Faith

Gwen Smith

Today's Truth

Then one of the synagogue leaders, named Jairus, came, and when he saw Jesus, he fell at his feet. He pleaded earnestly with him, "My little daughter is dying. Please come and put your hands on her so that she will be healed and live." (Mark 5:22–23)

Friend to Friend

I recently had a painful phone conversation with a girlfriend. She was heavy with hurt. Spiritually paralyzed by circumstances. Her faith had been greatly challenged and weakened. It broke my heart. I wanted to reach through the phone line and hug her. I wanted to lift her burdens and solve all her problems, but of course I couldn't. So I listened, reminded her of God's love for her, and prayed.

Are you feeling overwhelmed today? Discouraged by the complicated challenges you face? Or maybe life is going well for you right now, but you have a friend who is nursing emotional wounds. There are so many hurting hearts in this world. So many burdens being carried by souls weary of the task. So many people desperate for a miracle from God. Desperate for healing and hope.

God knew we would struggle with difficulties. So in His Word, He lovingly points us to hope. Back in the days of Jesus's ministry, a man who was desperate for a miracle approached Jesus and fell before Him. The man's daughter was dying. Jesus was his only hope. Here's how the scene plays out:

> After Jesus crossed over by boat, a large crowd met him at the seaside. One of the meeting-place leaders named Jairus came. When he saw Jesus, he fell to his knees, beside himself as he begged, "My dear daughter is at death's door. Come and lay hands on her so she will get well and live." Jesus went with him, the whole crowd tagging along, pushing and jostling him.… (Mark 5:21–24, MSG)

Along the way, Jesus healed a woman who had suffered from a bleeding disorder for twelve long years. Jesus said that her faith made her well.

> "Daughter, you took a risk of faith, and now you're healed and whole. Live well, lived blessed! Be healed of your plague."
>
> While he was still talking, some people came from the leader's house and told him, "Your daughter is dead. Why bother the Teacher any more?"
>
> Jesus overheard what they were talking about and said to the leader, "Don't listen to them; just trust me."
>
> He permitted no one to go in with him except Peter, James, and John. They entered the leader's house and pushed their way through the gossips looking for a story and neighbors bringing casseroles. Jesus was abrupt: "Why all this

busybody grief and gossip? This child isn't dead; she's sleeping." Provoked to sarcasm, they told him he didn't know what he was talking about.

But when he had sent them all out, he took the child's father and mother, along with his companions, and entered the child's room. He clasped the girl's hand and said, "Talitha koum," which means, "Little girl, get up." At that, she was up and walking around! This girl was twelve years of age. They, of course, were all beside themselves with joy. (Mark 5:34–42, MSG)

Desperate times call for desperate faith. As Christians, we have faith in a person—Jesus Christ. Faith in and of itself is meaningless, but faith in an all-seeing, all-knowing, all-powerful Savior means everything—because He is the same yesterday, today, and forever. Faith is the core of our lives. It is essential to pleasing God. He wants us to trust Him in every trial and through every trouble. "And without faith it is impossible to please God, because anyone who comes to him must believe that he exists and that he rewards those who earnestly seek him" (Hebrews 11:6).

Like Jairus and the bleeding woman, the best thing you can do is take your needs to Jesus. Purposefully place your faith in the Faithful One. When you fall before Him in prayer, He will sustain and strengthen you—but rest assured, if you try to handle things in your own strength, you will remain weak and ineffective.

Are you desperate for a miracle today? Is the declining economy, the burden of debt, or the soaring unemployment rate affecting you or someone you love? Perhaps you bear the pain of a broken marriage, broken dreams, or a broken body. If you are desperate for

healing, help, and hope, ask the Lord to increase your faith today, and make a determined choice to trust Him. When you do, He will meet you at your need and carry the load of your burdens for you.

Let's Pray

Heavenly Father, You are a mighty God, and I'm in need of Your power in my life. I beg You to move! Please fan the flame of my faith today. I trust that You are in control and ask that You would sustain and strengthen me to face every challenge. In Jesus's name I pray, amen.

A Place Called Home

Mary Southerland

Today's Truth

For this world is not our permanent home; we are looking forward to a home yet to come. (Hebrews 13:14, NLT)

Friend to Friend

It had been a wonderful evening with our daughter, Danna, and her sixteen-month-old son, Justus. We ate dinner at one of our favorite restaurants to celebrate Danna's graduation and the fact that we had all survived the grueling schedule her school had demanded. We laughed until we cried as Danna described her encounter that day with a teacher who seemed to be preoccupied with blue cornbread. I am not kidding! Justus may not have understood what his mom was saying, but he joined in the family celebration with gusto—laughing and clapping his little hands. After a delicious meal, we climbed into the car and headed home.

When we pulled into our neighborhood, Justus began clapping and pointing...at something. We were clueless until we pulled into the driveway. Our sweet little man laughed and bounced with excitement in his car seat. Justus was glad to be home.

At that precise moment, a line from one of my favorite movies, *Apollo 13,* popped into my mind. "Houston, we have a problem" may very well be one of the greatest understatements of all time. The astronauts longed for home and safety. They faced seemingly impossible odds of getting back to earth but refused to give up the fight until they splashed down in the waters of *home.*

We all long for a safe place to call home. When life brutally thrusts us into a world of fear and uncertainty, it is hard to trust God. Shaky circumstances rattle our faith. Relief seems like a remote possibility, and that light at the end of the tunnel is actually the headlight of another trial headed our way. The hits just keep coming, and we wonder if our world will ever be right again.

We all come into this world with a sense of being lost. Tucked into the corner of our souls is a feeling of restlessness…a longing for home, for something or someone eternal. That longing will never be satisfied outside of a personal relationship with Jesus Christ. He holds each today and every tomorrow in His hands. Nothing and no one but Jesus Christ can fill that God-shaped hole in our heart.

I have come to cherish that desperate cry of my heart that drives me to my knees and into the arms of God, my Father. Each and every time I come to Him, He whispers, "It will be all right. You are not home—yet."

No, this broken world is not my final home because I know God and He knows me. I have surrendered my life to Him and can face tomorrow because Jesus Christ lives. Yes, this world is just the beginning of the eternity for which I was created. I am just passing through, but while I am here, I have a God-size job to do, an extraordinary mission to complete, and a wonderful purpose to fulfill. So do you! It doesn't get any better than that, girlfriend.

As you dive into your hectic schedule, remember that one day

you will be home—with Him—but until then, trust God here and now. Guard your heart by filling it with God's Word. Hold fast to the true meaning of following God and don't let go! Look for ways to share the message of God's unconditional love. Embrace that longing for home and trust God to get you there.

Let's Pray

Father, I love You and am so thankful for the hope that life holds because I know You. I praise You and celebrate the truth that I am not alone, nor will I ever be. I will lack nothing because You are my Provider. I can sing in the midst of every storm because You are sufficient. I praise You and long for home, but until then, help me to be all that You created me to be. In Jesus's name, amen.

Now It's Your Turn

TIME FOR REFLECTION

- Got hope? Can you think of a friend who is discouraged and needs prayer? Call, e-mail, or send a card of encouragement to a friend who is hurting. Speak life and hope into her heart. Pray for her.
- Read Psalm 86:15: "But you, Lord, are a compassionate and gracious God, slow to anger, abounding in love and faithfulness."
  Write down the words in this verse that describe God.
  What do these words tell you about God's willingness to bless your life?
- What would have been your first thought if you were in a car accident like Gayle's and damaged the very knee you had been having trouble with for years? Be honest...and no hindsight allowed.
- How much time do you spend each morning—choosing a killer outfit to wear, applying makeup, and doing your hair—before you head out the door? We need to get ready to face trials too. The best way to *get ready* for the next trial is to *stay ready* for the next trial. In other words, now is the time to prepare your heart and mind for whatever trial lies ahead. Here are some tips to get you started:
  1. Make time each day to be alone with God.
  2. Pour out your dreams and desperation to Him.

3. Invest fifteen minutes in solitude each day, allowing your soul to "catch up."

4. Identify the top three joy thieves in your life and make a plan to eliminate them.

- Prayerfully choose five verses of Scripture about peace. Write these verses on index cards, carry them with you, and read them each time you are tempted to become frazzled. Consider making this idea a family project. Do this for a month and then evaluate the difference it has made in each person's ability to trust God in every difficult circumstance.

- Facing any giants? List three of the problems you are currently facing. Surrender each one to God and rest in His power and strength to make those giants fall.

1. _____

2. _____

3. _____

- The Bible tells us that when we are in spiritual battles, no weapon formed against us can prevail when we go in the power and strength of God (see Isaiah 54:17). When David remembered his past victories, his God-confidence was off the charts! We can gain God-confidence the same way. What battles has God brought you through in the past?

1. _____

2. _____

3. _____

Go, fight, win, girlfriend! When you remember the things that you have been brought through, a fresh God-confidence will rise up from deep within and give you courage to face whatever lies ahead.

- Wrap up your response time with prayer. Move from confession, to adoration, to thanksgiving, and end with your petitions (personal prayer needs.)

YOUR GiG TRUST ADVENTURE JOURNAL

Spend a few moments contemplating and journaling about some of the scriptural truths that moved your heart as you read the devotions this week. Then write a prayer of response to God.

_____

_____

_____

_____

_____

_____

_____

_____

_____

_____

_____

_____

*Come to me, all you who are weary and burdened, and I
will give you rest. Take my yoke upon you and learn from
me, for I am gentle and humble in heart, and you will find
rest for your souls. For my yoke is easy and my burden is light.
(Matthew 11:28–30)*

1

When We Don't Understand

Sharon Jaynes

Today's Truth

One thing God has spoken, two things I have heard: "Power belongs to you, God, and with you, Lord, is unfailing love." (Psalm 62:11–12)

Friend to Friend

"Mommy, Mommy!" Steven cried. "Don't let them hurt me!"

My son, Steven, was three years old when he contracted a severe case of the flu. He looked up at me with hollow eyes and slumped listlessly like a rag doll in my lap. When I carried my limp little one into the pediatrician's office, the doctor quickly surmised that Steven was dehydrated and needed to be admitted to the hospital immediately.

My heart broke as nurses strapped my baby boy onto a table and began to insert IV needles into his tiny arms. "Mommy, Mommy, help me!" he cried. "They're hurting me! Make them stop!"

"No, honey." I tried to reassure him through tears that matched

his own. "They're not trying to hurt you. They are going to make you all better."

Steven cried. I cried. The nurses cried.

I could only imagine what was going through Steven's little mind: *Why are these people hurting me? Why doesn't Mommy make them stop? She must not love me. She's not protecting me. If she loved me, she wouldn't let this happen. She must not care about me.*

Standing in the corner watching my little boy cry, I suddenly realized that God was giving me a glimpse into how He feels when I am going through a painful situation that is for my benefit. I cry out, *"Why are You letting this happen? Don't You love me? Don't You care about what's happening to me? Why don't You make it stop?"*

Sometimes you are like this little lamb, God seemed to say. *You don't understand the purpose of the pain, and you often think I have deserted you. But I will never leave you. You think that I don't love you, but I love you to the height of heaven and the depth of the sea. You think that I don't care about what's happening to you, but I am orchestrating your days and care about every hair on your head. My ways are higher than your ways, and My thoughts are higher than your thoughts. Yes, I do care about you and what is happening to you. I am bringing you to spiritual health and wholeness.*

Jesus promised that we would have struggles in this life (see John 16:33). James told us to "consider it pure joy" whenever we face trials "because you know that the testing of your faith produces perseverance. Let perseverance finish its work so that you may be mature and complete, not lacking anything" (James 1:2–4). Honestly, I wish there were some other way to learn the lessons God has for me. But just as Steven needed the IV fluid to nourish his dehydrated body, sometimes God uses the needles of difficulties and trials to allow the

lessons of life to enter through my tough exterior, flow through my languishing soul, and nourish my spirit to health and wholeness.

Like King David I often cry out, "My God, my God, why have you forsaken me? Why are you so far from saving me, from the words of my groaning?" (Psalm 22:1, ESV). And then I open my eyes to see that God was there all the time.

Even when we don't understand, when we can't see His plan, we can know that all His ways are loving and kind. He knows what's best for us, and He is always good.

If you are going through a difficult time right now—a circumstance that you don't understand—know that your heavenly Father is right by your side. He loves you dearly and sometimes allows painful situations to work for our ultimate good.

Let's Pray

Dear heavenly Father, I am so glad that You will never leave me. I'll admit that sometimes I whine, even cry, because I don't understand why You allow certain things to happen in my life. But I know that You are sovereign and that nothing happens by chance in the life of Your children. You are shaping and molding me into the woman You desire me to be. I trust You and Your ways even when I don't understand. In Jesus's name, amen.

2

When the Answer
Is No

Gwen Smith

Today's Truth

But he said to me, "My grace is sufficient for you, for my power is made perfect in weakness." Therefore I will boast all the more gladly about my weaknesses, so that Christ's power may rest on me. (2 Corinthians 12:9)

Friend to Friend

Karen was a godly woman who lost her battle against cancer. In spite of the medical struggles she faced and the pain that terrorized her body, Karen's faith was immovable. She knew God to be her "refuge and strength, a very present help in trouble" (Psalm 46:1, ESV). Her unwavering faith inspired a community of believers, as she held strong to the very end.

Though many prayed for Karen to be healed of cancer, God's answer was no. As she said good-bye to all she loved here on earth, Karen was comforted in knowing that she worshiped a risen Savior

who was familiar with suffering. She held tight to Jesus, and because she did, her life boasted of God's glory.

In the summer of 2002, Shira and Joey Arnold were delighted to learn that they were expecting their first child. They excitedly shared the news with family and friends as they began to plan for their new family. Weeks later, however, Shira and Joey got dream-shattering news. Routine tests at the doctor's office revealed that their baby was not developing correctly. The couple was advised by medical professionals to consider termination of the pregnancy. They adamantly refused.

Though Shira and Joey grieved deeply when they heard the news, they determined to trust in God and prayed for a miracle. Little Cayden was born blind, deaf, unable to walk, and with only half a brain. The doctors had expected him to live only minutes, but Cayden defied all odds by living just shy of five years. Five broken yet beautiful years. Five years filled with one struggle and one joy after another. Five years filled with miracles. Five glorious years.

During his short life on earth, through the wonders of modern medicine, technology, and prayers, Cayden learned to see, hear, speak, and walk. Those five medically complicated years were a constant challenge for the Arnolds, but God brought them through every difficult moment in His strength and allowed them to experience His joy, peace, and hope in spite of their challenges. He strengthened them with His grace.

Cayden's life was a beautifully broken display of God's glory. And though God's answer to their prayers for the complete healing of his tiny body here on earth was no, He provided both Cayden and his parents grace that was sufficient for each moment. For each day. For each weakness.

The funeral was a bittersweet, joy-filled celebration of Cayden's life. Shira and Joey honored God as their grace-giving, strength-supplying Strong Tower. The Arnolds spoke of their trust journey. They testified that they had to *choose* to trust God and readily admitted that it required constant choosing. They boasted in the Lord as David did in the Psalms when he delighted in God's strength:

> From the ends of the earth I call to you, I call as my heart
> grows faint; lead me to the rock that is higher than I. For
> you have been my refuge, a strong tower against the foe. I
> long to dwell in your tent forever and take refuge in the
> shelter of your wings. (Psalm 61:2–4)

It can be very frustrating to be told no. Many godly people in Scripture were told no. Moses was a man of great faith, but he wasn't allowed to set foot in the Promised Land. The apostle Paul was also told no by God. He knew suffering. He asked God three times to remove a "thorn in [his] flesh"—some sort of physical ailment that he ended up living with until his death (2 Corinthians 12:7). Even though God's answer was no, Paul's response was praise. He testified that he was strengthened by God's all-sufficient grace.

> Three times I pleaded with the Lord to take it away from
> me. But he said to me, "My grace is sufficient for you, for
> my power is made perfect in weakness." Therefore I will
> boast all the more gladly about my weaknesses, so that
> Christ's power may rest on me. That is why, for Christ's
> sake, I delight in weaknesses, in insults, in hardships, in
> persecutions, in difficulties. For when I am weak, then I
> am strong. (verses 8–10)

We all face challenges. Each trial is a trust opportunity. Each obstacle you encounter comes with a choice: Will you choose to trust in the power and sovereignty of God or will you choose to doubt?

Your life is purposed to bring glory to God in and through everything. There are times—hard times—when the answers from Him are no. When those times come, we need to choose to trust that He said no for a reason.

God is all-knowing. All-powerful.

We are not.

When we surrender to His sovereignty, God strengthens His children with His all-sufficient grace, and His power is made perfect in our weakness.

Let's Pray

Dear Lord, thank You for grace that strengthens me when I am weak. Your glory is my purpose. Help me to trust You in the challenges and the nos that I face today and every day. Shine Your glory through the cracks in my life today. In Jesus's name I pray, amen.

Life Scares Me

Mary Southerland

Today's Truth

But I will sing of your strength, in the morning I will sing of your love; for you are my fortress, my refuge in times of trouble. (Psalm 59:16)

Friend to Friend

I will never forget the first time I took our two-year-old son to the beach. I assumed Jered would take one look at the ocean and make a beeline for the water. We lived in South Florida, where many of the people we knew either had a swimming pool or lived on a canal that ran through their backyard. Since the tropical climate made it possible for Jered to play outside almost every day of the year, it was not unusual for him to be around water of some kind on a regular basis.

Just to be sure the trip was successful, I did what I thought was a fairly impressive job of preparing Jered for his first beach adventure. We talked and read books about the ocean and watched television shows about going to the beach. We quizzed friends about the best places to go once we got there and, finally, the day came when we actually went to the beach.

I am a list-maker and had compiled an extensive list of things to do and take with us:

Suntan lotion. Check.

Picnic basket filled with snacks and drinks. Check.

Mickey Mouse sunglasses and hat for Jered. Check.

Beach towels, a beach ball, and toys for building sand castles. Check.

Jered helped me pack the car and then scrambled into his car seat yelling, "Go, Mom! Hurry!" I did, and off we went. We sang and laughed all the way and planned what we were going to do once we reached the water. Honestly, it never crossed my mind that Jered would be afraid of the ocean because Jered is afraid of very little in life. Even as a toddler, he approached each task with confidence and the attitude that the only reason he could not do something was because he had not had the opportunity to try.

As we pulled into an oceanfront parking lot, Jered began clapping and cheering. He quickly scrambled out of his car seat, grabbed my hand, and promptly froze. Miles of sand and water stretched out before him in every direction. When the waves crashed against the sand, he gripped my hand and asked, "What's that, Mom?"

Puzzled, I said, "Why, that is the ocean, honey. Isn't it great?" I watched the color drain out of my son's face as he backed up, pulling me with him.

"I don't want beach, Mom!" I couldn't believe it! Obviously a little reassurance was needed. When I pulled Jered into my arms and slowly edged my way toward the water, he promptly burst into tears. "Too big, Mommy! Too big!" he cried. I suddenly realized that Jered did indeed love the water—as long as it was surrounded by cement and filled with chlorine. The ocean was an entirely different matter altogether. It was too big and completely overwhelming.

Are you facing a circumstance that is much too big for you to handle? The deafening waves of doubt may be crashing around you, drowning out the promises of God. The unknown stretches before you, and all you can see are the mistakes you have made and the opportunities you have missed. Fear has brought you to your knees and you are more desperate than you have ever been in your life. The questions far outnumber the answers. You cry alone in a darkness that is unlike any you have ever faced. You long to be understood, and crave a love that accepts you just as you are in the midst of your fear and doubt.

I have great news for you, girlfriend! God sees you. He has not been caught off guard by the circumstances you face, and where you are is no surprise to Him. In fact, God will take what the Enemy means for evil and use it as the perfect setting for a miracle. You don't have to understand God to trust Him. Restoration and peace are His specialty. He will be your refuge and your strength. Right now, quietly turn to Him. He is waiting.

Let's Pray

Father, I come to You today with a sense of helplessness. I am desperate for You, Lord. I need Your strength and power to sustain me because everything seems to be falling apart. I want to be a woman of faith and stand strong when trouble bombards my life, but I cannot do it alone. Today, I turn to You, God, and celebrate the truth that You will turn to me and be my refuge. In Jesus's name, amen.

A Little Child Shall Lead Them

Sharon Jaynes

Today's Truth

A little child will lead them. (Isaiah 11:6)

Friend to Friend

As I look at the happy faces of our little Jaynes threesome smiling back at me from various pictures around our family room, I'm reminded that God's plans and our plans are not always the same.

When my husband, Steve, and I decided to have children, we conceived with no problem. Steven Hugh Jaynes Jr. was born with a shock of thick black hair and long Bambi-like eyelashes that had the nurses measuring for record-breaking length. I loved being a mother more than any role I had ever experienced. Never in my life had I ever imagined so much love could be wrapped in such a small package.

Steven was about two years old when we decided to expand our family once again.

"Steven," we explained, "we are praying that God will give

Mommy and Daddy another Jaynes baby so you can have a little brother or sister."

He thought that sounded like a good idea, so he ended our family prayer time each night with the benediction, "And, God, please give Mommy and Daddy another Jaynes baby. Amen."

After six months, there was no news of another Jaynes baby. I was perplexed. Then a year passed with no news. I was distraught. Then two years passed with no signs of another child on the way. I began sinking in a sea of fear and doubt. All the while Steven prayed each night, "And, God, please give Mommy and Daddy another Jaynes baby."

Steve and I began traveling down the frustrating road of doctor visits, infertility treatment, and timed intimacy (which is anything but intimate). Then I began worrying about how this "unanswered" prayer was going to affect Steven's faith in God.

Steven was approaching five years old, and we still had no news. Apparently, it was not the Lord's desire for us to have another child at this time, and I didn't know how to tell Steven that he didn't have to pray that prayer every night. I kept hoping that he would just forget about it. But he didn't forget about it any more than he forgot the "amen" at the end. So I began to pray, *Lord, please show me how to ease out of this predicament. Show me how to tell Steven that we don't need to pray for another baby every night. I do not want this seemingly unanswered prayer to damage his faith.*

We had a miniature table and chairs in the kitchen where Steven and I ate lunch together each day. One day, while sharing peanut butter and jelly sandwiches, Steven looked up and, in his sweet little voice, said, "Mommy, have you ever thought that maybe God only wants you to have one Jaynes baby?"

Shocked, I answered, "Yes, I have thought that maybe that is the

case, and if it is, I am so thankful because He has given me all I have ever hoped for in a child wrapped up in one package. You!"

Then he turned his little head like a robin and said, "Well, what I think we ought to do is keep praying until you're too old to have one. Then we'll know that's His answer!"

What a great idea! I had been worried about Steven's faith, but all the while, it was my own that was suffering. I was having trouble believing that God loved me when He was withholding what I wanted most—a houseful of children. *How could He love me and not give me the desire of my heart?* I wondered. *Maybe He doesn't love me after all.*

Steven didn't know how old too old was, but he did trust God. He knew God could do anything. If His answer was no, he didn't have a problem with that. I had told him no many times, and he understood that no did not mean "I don't love you." No just meant "No, because I am your mom, and I know what's best for you." Likewise, if God says no to me, it is not because He doesn't love me, but because He is my Father who knows what is best for me.

God is not like a benevolent grandfather who gives his children whatever they want. Rather, He is a loving Father who always does what is best for His children so that we can become well-disciplined offspring who are conformed to the image of Christ. And like a good father, sometimes that means saying yes and sometimes it means saying no.

The Lord taught me a great lesson through my little boy. Through Steven's childlike faith, I saw an example of the trust I should have toward my heavenly Father who loves me and knows what's best for me—even when I don't understand. No matter what you are going through today, know this: God is your heavenly Father who knows what's best for you, and you can trust Him.

Let's Pray

Dear Father, I know You answer every one of my prayers. Help me to accept when Your answer is no. I trust You and believe that You know what is best for me, even when I don't understand. In Jesus's name, amen.

Between Faith and a Hard Place

Gwen Smith

Today's Truth

The LORD is close to the brokenhearted and saves those who are crushed in spirit. (Psalm 34:18)

Friend to Friend

Nineteenth-century preacher C. H. Spurgeon wrote in his devotional book *Morning and Evening:*

> God often sends us trials that our graces may be discovered, and that we may be certified of their existence. Besides, it is not merely discovery, real growth in grace is the result of sanctified trials. God often takes away our comforts and our privileges in order to make us better Christians. He trains His soldiers, not in tents of ease and luxury, but by turning them out to forced marches and hard service. He makes them ford through streams, and swim through rivers, and climb mountains, and walk many a long mile with heavy

knapsacks of sorrow on their backs. Well, Christian, may not
this account for the troubles through which thou art passing?
Is not the Lord bringing out your graces, and making them
grow? Is not this the reason why He is contending with you?

Like Spurgeon, the Bible tells us hard truths. It doesn't paint a
rosy picture. It actually paints a thorny picture. It promises hardship.
It assures us that in this life there will be troubles, times when we find
ourselves caught between faith and a hard place.

Christianity is no free lunch. Faith in Christ doesn't shield us
from troubles, but it does help us through them. There are natural
tensions here. Questions that beg to be asked:

Is God really all loving? Yes.

Is God always good? Yes.

Will we each find ourselves caught between faith and hard
places? Yes.

Many television preachers, churches, and groups will tell you
differently, but the truth remains: faith is an anchor of hope for the
believer. Trusting God is a core essential. Jesus said, "I am the vine;
you are the branches. If you remain in me and I in you, you will bear
much fruit; apart from me you can do nothing" (John 15:5). Jesus
also spoke of the hard times we would face. "I have told you these
things, so that in me you may have peace. In this world you will have
trouble. But take heart! I have overcome the world" (John 16:33).

We may not have all the answers to life's hard questions, and we
may not know why God's hand brings healing to some and not to
others, but we do know that when we take our burdens to Jesus, we
can experience peace in each hard place. "Peace I leave with you; my
peace I give to you. Not as the world gives do I give to you. Let not
your hearts be troubled, neither let them be afraid" (John 14:27,

ESV). Our Lord is always faithful, whether we are delivered *from* our hard places or *through* them.

"The LORD is close to the brokenhearted and saves those who are crushed in spirit" (Psalm 34:18). I'm not sure what hard places you face today, but God knows exactly where you are and what you're facing. When you find yourself between faith and a hard place, even in the times when you don't know what to pray, turn to the Lord. Choose to trust Him. God hears every cry and loves you deeply.

> Trust in the LORD with all your heart
>> and do not lean on your own understanding.
> In all your ways acknowledge Him,
>> and He will make your paths straight.
>> (Proverbs 3:5–6, NASB)

Let's Pray

Dear Lord, thanks for the reminder that I never have to walk through a trial without You. Help me to trust You in everything, even when I don't understand. Today, I bring _____ to You and ask that You would move powerfully in and through this burden of my heart, whether You choose in Your sovereignty to remove it or work through it. In Jesus's name, amen.

Now It's Your Turn

TIME FOR REFLECTION

- Have you ever had to help someone by doing something that was painful to them? (Like pour peroxide on a wound or help someone with physical therapy.) If so, how did it make you feel to watch them experience pain?

    Did you persist with helping? If so, why? What was the outcome?

- How can you relate that to how God must feel when we are experiencing pain that is for our ultimate good?

- Look back over your life. When did God take something bad and bring good out of it? Describe that experience.

- One of the devotions this week took us to the ocean. (Yay! Field trip!) Are your current life struggles the size of a swimming pool, a lake, or an ocean?

- Even though the size of our trust-challenges changes, the Faithful One never does. Read Hebrews 13:8: "Jesus Christ is the same yesterday and today and forever." Discuss why this unchanging truth matters in the midst of our constantly changing struggles.

- Read aloud these verses from Psalm 34:

I sought the LORD, and he answered me;
> he delivered me from all my fears.

Those who look to him are radiant;
> their faces are never covered with shame.

This poor man called, and the LORD heard him;
> he saved him out of all his troubles.

The angel of the LORD encamps around those who fear him,
> and he delivers them.

Taste and see that the LORD is good;
> blessed is the one who takes refuge in him.

Fear the LORD, you his holy people,
> for those who fear him lack nothing.

The lions may grow weak and hungry,
> but those who seek the LORD lack no good thing.

Come, my children, listen to me;
> I will teach you the fear of the LORD.

Whoever of you loves life
> and desires to see many good days,

keep your tongue from evil
> and your lips from telling lies.

Turn from evil and do good;
> seek peace and pursue it.

The eyes of the LORD are on the righteous,
> and his ears are attentive to their cry;

but the face of the LORD is against those who do evil,
> to blot out their name from the earth.

The righteous cry out, and the LORD hears them;
> he delivers them from all their troubles.

The LORD is close to the brokenhearted
> and saves those who are crushed in spirit.

The righteous person may have many troubles,
> but the LORD delivers him from them all.
>> (verses 4–19)

> Was there a verse that jumped out at you and spoke to
> your heart? If so, which one(s) and why?

- Sharon told a story this week of a beautiful faith lesson that God taught her through her son, Steven, and through His answer of no. Suppose God said yes to every one of our prayer requests. Boy, what a mess we would have! Can you think of two or three prayers that you are so glad God's answer was no? (Oh, to be a fly on the wall of your discussion!)

- In the New Testament book of John, Jesus talked to His disciples about "remaining" in Him: "Remain in me, as I also remain in you. No branch can bear fruit by itself; it must remain in the vine. Neither can you bear fruit unless you remain in me. I am the vine; you are the branches. If you remain in me and I in you, you will bear much fruit; apart from me you can do nothing" (15:4–5).

> What do you think Jesus meant when He told us to
> remain in Him? Throw some real life on it: What
> does that look like in the midst of busy days? What
> would the fruit look like?

- Wrap up your response time with prayer. Move from confession, to adoration, to thanksgiving, and end with your petitions (personal prayer needs).

YOUR GIG TRUST ADVENTURE JOURNAL

Spend a few moments contemplating and journaling about some of the scriptural truths that moved your heart as you read the devotions this week. Then write a prayer of response to God.

_____

_____

_____

_____

_____

_____

_____

_____

_____

_____

_____

_____

_____

_____

_____

_____

_____

_____

_____

_____

_____

_____

_____

_____

_____

_____

_____

_____

_____

_____

But I will sing of your strength, in the morning I will sing of your love; for you are my fortress, my refuge in times of trouble. (Psalm 59:16)

Who Do You Think You Are?

Sharon Jaynes

Today's Truth

Such confidence we have through Christ before God. Not that we are competent in ourselves to claim anything for ourselves, but our competence comes from God. (2 Corinthians 3:4–5)

Friend to Friend

It was my first big speaking engagement before a large group of women, and I was terrified. Ironically, my topic was "Unshakable Confidence in Christ."

Two weeks before I was to speak to the group, I attended a luncheon. As soon as I walked into the lovely Southern estate, I felt old insecurities begin to bubble up. Two ladies whom I did not know were sitting at my table, and they were talking about a speaker they had recently heard at the church where I would be speaking in a few weeks.

"He was the most powerful speaker I have ever heard," one said.

"I cried all the way through his testimony. Just to think, he had

to live with the fact that his son was an arsonist. Oh, how God has worked mightily in the family. The pastor was so moved that he asked the speaker to preach at the Sunday night service. That is highly unusual. I don't think we will ever have a speaker that good again."

On and on they went, singing the praises of this mighty man of God. They used words like *dynamic, powerful, electric,* and *eloquent.* I never mentioned that I would be the speaker for their next meeting. At that point, I wasn't so sure I would be.

As I listened to the ladies, my throat constricted, the tea sandwiches clung to the roof of my mouth, and my heart pounded wildly. Then Satan, the gatekeeper of the three-headed monster of inferiority, insecurity, and inadequacy, let him out. The monster came screaming my way hurling accusations that sounded all too familiar.

"Who do you think you are, going to speak at this event? Listen to the caliber of people they bring in. This man came from all the way across the country. You are coming from just across town. What could you possibly have to say to help these women? If I were you, I'd bow out now before you embarrass yourself."

You know what? Even though I knew it was the Enemy speaking lies in my soul, I started to believe him. After all, what he was saying made a lot more sense than the "Who I am in Christ" statements posted on my refrigerator door.

After the luncheon, I decided to go by the church and purchase a tape of the previous speaker, just to see what I was going to be compared to. I walked into the church, paid my five dollars, popped the tape in the console, and braced myself for the hour of power.

Nothing happened.

I fast forwarded the tape.

Nothing happened.

I flipped the tape over.

Nothing happened. The tape was blank.

At that moment, I did not hear the dynamic speaker on the tape; I heard God speak to my heart.

Sharon, you do not need to hear what My servant said to these people two weeks ago. The tape is blank because I do not want you to compare yourself to anyone else. It doesn't matter what he said. I will give you a message for these ladies. I can speak through a prophet, I can speak through a fisherman, and I can speak through a donkey.

I gave him a message, and I have given you one as well. Who are you "performing" for, My child, them or Me? Do not compare yourself to anyone. You are my child, and I am asking you to speak to an audience of One.

It was indeed an hour of power. I didn't bother getting my money back for the defective tape. It was exactly what I needed to hear.

It was really a matter of trust. Did I trust God to speak through me, or was I afraid He wasn't going to show up? Did I trust God to give me the message, or was I afraid that He would leave me blubbering behind the mic? Did I trust God to give me the power of the Holy Spirit to minister to the women, or was I afraid? I decided to trust God.

So the next time Satan said to me, "Who do you think you are?" let me tell you what I told him. "I am the light of the world. I am the salt of the earth. I am a child of God. I am the bride of Christ. I am a joint heir with Christ. I have the power of the Holy Spirit. I have been delivered from the domain of darkness and transferred to the kingdom of Christ. I am chosen of God, holy and dearly loved. And who are you?"

Are you listening to the Enemy who says you can't do anything right, you're a loser, you're not good enough? Or are you listening to God who says you are a chosen, holy, dearly loved child who is equipped by God, empowered by the Holy Spirit, and enveloped by Jesus Christ? Let's believe God today!

Let's Pray

Dear God, I know that without You I am nothing but an empty vessel. However, because of You, I am filled with the power of the Holy Spirit and have been blessed with every spiritual blessing! I can be confident because of who I am as a child of the King. I can do everything through Christ who strengthens me! In Jesus's name, amen.

The Wrestling Match

Gwen Smith

Today's Truth

Finally, be strong in the Lord and in his mighty power. Put on the full armor of God, so that you can take your stand against the devil's schemes. For our struggle is not against flesh and blood, but against the rulers, against the authorities, against the powers of this dark world and against the spiritual forces of evil in the heavenly realms. (Ephesians 6:10–12)

Friend to Friend

It was the end of the school year. The sun was blazing in the sweltering high 80s with not a hint of shade to be found on the treeless playground. The boys were stinky from their sweaty schoolyard endeavors, and the girls were now wilted versions of the fresh flowers they had been that morning. It was almost time for the big wrestling competition. Electric excitement lingered in the air. I was a fifth grader at West Hempfield Elementary School in Irwin, Pennsylvania, and I had signed up to participate in the wrestling match.

To this day, I'm somewhat amused and perplexed that I would've thrown myself into the middle of such a barbaric display. Wrestling

certainly wasn't my sport of choice or even a faint interest of mine. So, as we all gathered around the red-and-white-striped gymnasium mats for the annual end-of-the year wrestling tournament, I was sweating bullets—not just from the relentless, yellow ball of fire in the sky but also from the nerves that consumed my body.

Before the match even began, I was a captive to the bully in my brain, the bully that tried to steal my faith in my own abilities. *What do you think you are doing? This is ridiculous! Caroline is not only three inches taller than you, but she's meaner than you—and she's in the sixth grade! You are going down, Gwen. Prepare to be humiliated in front of every fourth, fifth, and sixth grader in the school.*

At the sound of the whistle, the match was on. Caroline and I danced around like two alley cats with their backs raised high. She had a confidence in her eye that was foreign to me at that moment. A series of unskilled and ungraceful moves followed. (Cringe with me here!) She lunged and I retreated. I lunged and she retreated. Then came contact. Within seconds we were on our hands and knees battling for control. Battling for the win.

The sounds of the crowd were deafening as Caroline moved in to get the better of me. All I could think was, *Just don't let her get you on your back!* Feelings of hopelessness and desperation flooded my heart as she and I exchanged move for move. There were several points allotted, and Mr. Gordon's whistle prompted several restarts. In the midst of this primitive battle, my goal had changed from trying to win to just trying *not* to be pinned. And therein lies the defeat.

As the match came to an end and the final whistle blew, it was Caroline's victorious arm that was raised high in the sky. I was defeated in front of half the school. Cheers went up for Caroline as I shrunk back into the sea of students, longing for superpowers that

would render me invisible. I was exhausted from the match, humiliated from my failure, and defeated by both Caroline and the voice in
my own mind.

That was a dark day for me as a young girl. But as dark as that
day was emotionally, I was able to clearly see my opponent. Friend,
when it comes to spiritual wrestling matches, we do not have the
advantage of sight. The Bible says: "Our struggle is not against flesh
and blood, but against the rulers, against the authorities, against the
powers of this dark world and against the spiritual forces of evil in
the heavenly realms" (Ephesians 6:12).

Many of the battles we contend with each day are spiritual. During the wrestling match, my focus switched from trying to win to
trying not to lose. The same thing often happens in our life struggles.
We try not to lose instead of pressing on to win, yet the Bible tells us
that we—who are in Christ—can stand each day assured of victory
when we call on the power of God. And at the heart of every spiritual
battle is a question: Will we choose to trust in the faithful God who
sees our opponent and promises to be our Strength, or will we suc-
cumb to our Enemy, who seeks to erode our trust in God so that he
may destroy us? We can't see our Enemy. And while at first glance
this may seem disarming, look again at Ephesians 6. The Bible
clearly tells us that we can be equipped to stand firm with the armor
of God!

> Therefore put on the full armor of God, so that when the day
> of evil comes, you may be able to stand your ground, and
> after you have done everything, to stand. Stand firm then,
> with the belt of truth buckled around your waist, with the
> breastplate of righteousness in place, and with your feet fitted
> with the readiness that comes from the gospel of peace. In

addition to all this, take up the shield of faith, with which
you can extinguish all the flaming arrows of the evil one.
Take the helmet of salvation and the sword of the Spirit,
which is the word of God. And pray in the Spirit on all
occasions with all kinds of prayers and requests. With this
in mind, be alert and always keep on praying for all the
Lord's people. (Ephesians 6:13–18)

Though the wrestling match with Caroline seemed overwhelm-
ingly daunting, the battles that I face now are so much greater. I'm
thankful that God's Word clearly says the victory is ours if we are in
Christ. If God is for us, who can be against us? Do we trust in this
truth?

What are you wrestling with today? Is the Enemy speaking lies
to you? Do you feel weak? Strength comes when we call on Jesus and
trust in Him! We can stand firm against the schemes of the devil
when we put on the armor of God! Suit up, girls! A battle rages on all
around you. Be strong in the Lord and in His mighty power!

Let's Pray

*Dear Lord, I thank You for being a mighty God who longs to cover my
weakness with Your strength. Please equip me for all that lies ahead
today, protect me from attacks and schemes of the Enemy, and help me
be strong in Your mighty power. Help me trust that You will cover me
with Your peace, truth, faith, and salvation so I can stand firm in the
battle. I ask this in the powerful name of Jesus, amen.*

Just Say Yes

Mary Southerland

Today's Truth

The one who calls you is faithful, and he will do it. (1 Thessalonians 5:24)

Friend to Friend

Hamburgers are a regular item on the Southerland summer menu for several reasons: they are inexpensive, easy to prepare, and scrumptious. But until last week I never considered hamburgers to be dangerous.

We live in Kansas, where the summer heat can be brutal. Why add to the rising temperature outside by turning on an oven inside? It was definitely a hamburger kind of night.

My husband offered to do the grilling, but he had just gotten home from work and looked like he needed sleep more than he needed to grill hamburgers. Being the wonderful wife that I am, I said, "Honey, why don't you take a quick nap while I cook dinner?" Being the wonderful husband that he is, Dan responded, "I'll be glad to do the grilling for you. It's really hot outside." I should have taken him up on his offer.

I didn't want to be in the scorching heat one minute longer than I had to be, so I quickly seasoned the hamburger patties, slapped them on the grill, and headed back in to set the table. I still had several things to do while the burgers cooked, but I got a better offer. My grandson wanted to play. I lost track of time and forgot the meal in progress on the grill. When our daughter asked what we were having for dinner, visions of charred hamburger patties danced through my head as I made a mad dash to rescue our meal.

I breathed a sigh of relief when I saw that the hamburgers were still edible—barely—but a little charcoal is a healthy addition to any diet, right? I quickly transferred the hamburgers to a plate, closed the lid on the grill, and turned to head inside. My foot caught on the leg of a patio chair, and I stumbled as I juggled the plate of meat in my hand. I was not about to give up those hamburgers without a fight. Instinctively, I reached out for something to break my fall and found the grill—with three fingers. I could feel the searing heat followed by the temporary numbness that accompanies second- and third-degree burns. I raced into the house where I immediately submerged the injured fingers into a bowl of ice water, but when large blisters began to appear, Dan and I headed to the nearby Urgent Care.

The doctor prescribed a cream that she promised would work wonders on the burns. "Will it stop the pain?" I asked because they had taken my bowl of ice water away, and I could not believe how much pain three little burned fingers could feel.

"It won't help with the pain as much as it will help the burns heal, but you will need a powerful painkiller," she replied, handing me a prescription for the same pain medication I had once taken after major surgery. I am not a doctor, but taking pain medication that affects the whole body seems like overkill when only three fingers are in pain. But as the hours passed, I was very thankful for each

little pill. I am pretty strong when it comes to dealing with pain, but I have to tell you that every part of my body was screaming, "Pay attention to the fingers! They hurt!"

The body of Christ should function the same way.

When someone hurts, we should respond to their pain. When one of us is weak, another should be strong. Those who stumble and fall should be able to count on someone to pick them up and finish the race. Instead, we often shoot our wounded and leave them lying in the dirt to find help on their own.

Admittedly, the problem is not always that we are unwilling to help someone in pain. We overlook hurting people because we are in a hurry or maybe we just don't want to deal with the mess of broken lives. Or maybe we are afraid of failure and rejection. It is essential that we remember: if God calls us to do something, He will give us everything we need to do it—if we trust Him and are willing to step out in faith. Jesus did.

Jesus willingly left His throne in heaven and came to earth as a man. He felt every pain we have ever felt or ever will feel. He was afraid and lonely and often had "no place to lay his head" (Matthew 8:20). Jesus was misunderstood and slandered and then crucified to pay for our sin. It must break the heart of God when we so easily toss aside what cost Him so much because we are afraid to trust Him and just say, "Yes, Lord."

Look around you, girlfriend. Someone needs you to acknowledge their pain and be willing to do something about it. Just say yes, and God will show you the next step.

Let's Pray

Father, forgive me for the times I could have made a difference in the life of someone who was hurting, but I didn't because I was too busy or just

didn't care enough. I lay my fear of failure at Your feet and trust You to provide everything I need to obey You. Break my heart so that I will see the needs of people around me. Right now, I say yes to whatever You ask me to do. In Jesus's name, amen.

Laughing in the Face of Fear

Sharon Jaynes

Today's Truth

So do not fear, for I am with you; do not be dismayed, for I am your God. (Isaiah 41:10)

Friend to Friend

Twenty tourists piled into a small boat to meander down the lazy river in the fantasy world of Universal Studios. We were in the make-believe town of Amity, where the man-eating shark of *Jaws* terrorized vacationers and made us all afraid to go in the water in the 1980s. In our tour boat, we slowly drifted along the calm canal when suddenly the waters began to stir. *Oh no! What was it?* Suddenly our greatest fears were realized! A giant shark erupted from the water and attacked our boat! It gnashed its teeth and lunged at the side of the boat. Women screamed, babies cried, and one hefty, overalls-clad man in the back of the boat just burst out laughing. Soon his contagious laughter caused an avalanche of giggles throughout the boat, and we all began laughing hysterically!

After much chomping, Jaws withdrew his fearsome fury and disappeared beneath the surface. But would it reappear? Were we safe? No! A few moments later, the mammoth shark emerged and lunged at our helpless vessel once again. And with each of the four times that shark appeared and attacked our boat, the laughing man had the same effect—contagious, side-splitting, rip-roaring laughter. Tears streamed down my face in uncontrollable cackling. I'm not sure the tour guide had ever seen anything like it.

See, the man knew that the shark was a fake. It wasn't real, so to him, the attack was…well, funny.

David was a young man who also laughed in the face of fear. When he was yet a teenage shepherd, he went to check on his big brothers, who were out at war. When he arrived on the battlefield, he noticed the entire Israelite army shaking in their sandals because of an enemy giant named Goliath who taunted them night and day.

"Who is this uncircumcised Philistine that he should defy the armies of the living God?" David asked (1 Samuel 17:26). "What's the problem? He's just a big fake. Don't worry. I'll fight him."

"You can't fight this giant!" the king responded. "You're just a boy, and this giant has been fighting men all his life!"

"The LORD who rescued me from the paw of the lion and the paw of the bear will rescue me from the hand of this Philistine," David replied (verse 37).

So David gathered five smooth stones and put them in the pouch of his shepherd's bag. As he ran toward the giant, he yelled, "You come against me with sword and spear and javelin, but I come against you in the name of the LORD Almighty, the God of the armies of Israel, whom you have defied.… All those gathered here will know that it is not by sword or spear that the LORD saves; for the battle is the LORD's, and he will give all of you into our hands" (verses 45, 47).

David put a rock in the sling and let it fly. The rock landed squarely in the middle of the giant's forehead, and he fell face forward—dead. Last time I checked, if someone gets hit in the forehead, he should fall backward. Goliath fell forward. Why? I think it is because David threw the stone but God killed the giant and pushed him over! (See 1 Samuel 17 for the entire amazing story.)

Jaws? I'm not worried. Giants? They're nothing compared to our almighty God. What about you? Are you allowing your fears to get the best of you, or allowing the best of you to trust in God?

Let's Pray

Dear God, I did it again. I got all worried and anxious about something that hasn't happened and probably never will. Help me to choose faith over fear, confidence over cowardice, and power over panic. In Jesus's name, amen.

Nothing Is Impossible with God

Gwen Smith

Today's Truth

Then Moses stretched out his hand over the sea, and all that night the LORD drove the sea back with a strong east wind and turned it into dry land. The waters were divided, and the Israelites went through the sea on dry ground, with a wall of water on their right and on their left. (Exodus 14:21–22)

Friend to Friend

A boy was sitting on a park bench with one hand resting on an open Bible. He was loudly exclaiming his praise to God. "Hallelujah! Hallelujah! God is great!" he yelled without worrying whether anyone heard him or not.

Shortly after, along came a man who had recently completed some studies at a local university. Feeling himself very enlightened in the ways of truth and very eager to show off his enlightenment, he asked the boy about the source of his joy.

"Hey," said the boy, "don't you have any idea what God is able to do? I just read that God opened up the waves of the Red Sea and led the whole nation of Israel right through the middle."

The enlightened man laughed lightly, sat down next to the boy, and began to try to open his eyes to the "realities" of the miracles recorded in the Bible. "That can all be very easily explained. Modern scholars have shown, for instance, that the Red Sea in that area was only ten inches deep at that time. It was no problem for the Israelites to wade across."

The boy was stumped. His eyes wandered from the man back to the Bible lying open in his lap. The man, content that he had enlightened a poor, naive young person as to the finer points of scientific insight, turned to go. He had taken only two steps when the boy began to rejoice and praise God louder than before. The man turned to ask the reason for this resumed jubilation.

"Wow!" exclaimed the boy happily. "God is greater than I thought! Not only did He lead the whole nation of Israel through the Red Sea, He topped it off by drowning the whole Egyptian army in ten inches of water!"

The Old Testament book of Exodus shows, over and over again, that nothing is impossible with God. Nothing! Moses was an ordinary man who was chosen by God to do an extraordinary task. On the far side of the desert in Midian, high on the mountain of God, Moses met the Lord face to flame. God appeared to Moses "in flames of fire from within a bush" (Exodus 3:2).

I would imagine that Moses was probably dirty, sweaty, and stinky from shepherding as he stood on holy ground before the Lord. I'm sure he was keenly aware of his filth and stench, both physical and spiritual. As he slipped off his shoes, he hid his face in fear.

Moses did not feel adequate for the assignment that he had been given. He wasn't confident about his ability to get the job done. In fact, he even pleaded with God to send someone else! Moses said to God, "Oh, my Lord, I am not eloquent, either in the past or since you have spoken to your servant, but I am slow of speech and of tongue" (Exodus 4:10, esv).

But God had a plan, and Moses was His man. Throughout ten plagues and many signs and wonders, God flexed His muscles through His servant Moses. Once Pharaoh had finally let God's people go, Moses led the Israelites out of Egypt. No compass was necessary. God led His people through the desert with a pillar of cloud by day and a pillar of fire by night. It must have been an amazing sight. It must have been thrilling...up until the point where Pharaoh's army was closing in on the Israelite people as they approached the Red Sea. Talk about being faced with a seemingly impossible situation! Moses and around two million of his closest Hebrew friends stood at the edge of the water with nowhere to go. They were trapped: "They were terrified and cried out to the LORD" (Exodus 14:10). *But God!* God was on time for the miracle show. He had a plan. He made a way. Nothing is too difficult for God!

> Moses answered the people, "Do not be afraid. Stand firm
> and you will see the deliverance the LORD will bring you
> today.... The LORD will fight for you; you need only to be
> still." (verses 13–14)

God purposed this extravagant rescue for His glory. The Lord fought for Israel, and He will fight for you as well. When God is on our side, when He is fighting for us, we can be assured of victory! And that's exactly what the nation of Israel experienced:

Then Moses stretched out his hand over the sea, and all that night the LORD drove the sea back with a strong east wind and turned it into dry land. The waters were divided, and the Israelites went through the sea on dry ground, with a wall of water on their right and on their left. (verses 21–22)

The Israelites were saved, and Pharaoh's army was destroyed—all under the watchful eyes of the Lord. God wanted to be glorified through a seemingly impossible situation. He wants to be glorified through the difficult situations that you face too. "If God is for us, who can be against us?" (Romans 8:31). When we stand with Christ, we stand with power.

What Red Sea are you facing? Nothing is impossible with God. When you set aside your doubts and call on the name of the Lord, you can face the stormy waters of your circumstances with a strong confidence, knowing that God is able and willing to do great things in and through you. Continue to follow the pillars of cloud and fire of God's leading. You have a chance to bring God the glory of which He is so deserving!

Let's Pray

Dear God, like Moses I often feel unequipped to handle the assignments You have given me. You know exactly what overwhelming waters I face today. As I stand at the water's edge, I commit to trusting Your strength. I will not give in to the fears, frustrations, and doubts that mock me. You are far more powerful than the circumstances of my life. Thank You for reminding me that nothing is too difficult for You. In Jesus's name, amen.

Now It's Your Turn

TIME FOR REFLECTION

- Imagine that there is an official tug-of-war match going on in your mind. On one side of a thick rope is the "team of lies" that tells you that you aren't good enough, that you can't do anything right, and that you are not significant. On the other side of the rope is the "team of truth" that tells you who you are in Christ: empowered, forgiven, equipped, free, valued, and purposed. On most days, which team wins the tug-of-war in your mind?

- Look up the following verses and write who the Lord says you are. (If you are discussing these questions with a friend or GiG group, split up the work and share the answers.) Example: Matthew 5:13: "salt of the earth."

  Matthew 5:13–14; 6:26

  John 14:20; 15:5, 15–16

  Romans 5:9–10; 8:2, 17, 37; 15:7

  1 Corinthians 2:16; 3:16; 6:11, 19; 12:27

  2 Corinthians 2:15; 5:17, 20-21

Galatians 3:13; 4:7

Ephesians 1:1, 3–5, 7, 11, 13; 2:5, 10, 19

Philippians 3:20; 4:13

Colossians 1:13, 22; 2:10; 3:13

1 Peter 2:9

1 John 1:9; 3:1–2

- Which of the above identity truths would be most beneficial for you to remind yourself of regularly? Select three and write them in a personal statement. For example: "I am God's chosen and royal daughter—His special possession!" (see 1 Peter 2:9).

  1. _____

  2. _____

  3. _____

- What is the biggest lie that you contend with regularly?
- Read Ephesians 6:13–17: "Therefore put on the full armor of God, so that when the day of evil comes, you may be able to stand your ground, and after you have done everything, to stand. Stand firm then, with the belt of truth buckled around your waist, with the breastplate of righteousness in place, and with your feet fitted with the readiness that comes from the gospel of peace. In addition to all this, take up the shield of faith, with which you can extinguish all the flaming arrows of the evil one. Take the helmet of salvation and the sword of the Spirit, which is the word of God."

Fill in phrases below with the armor of God soul-equipment that we should put on each day.

1. Belt of _____

2. Breastplate of _____

3. Shoes of _____

4. Shield of _____

5. Helmet of _____

6. Sword of the _____

- What "invisible enemies" are you currently wrestling with? (For example: doubt, fear, insecurity...)
- How could your days and your "invisible enemies" be affected by praying for and believing the Lord to equip you with His armor?
- Do you think that suiting up in God's armor will increase your willingness to trust God? Why or why not?
- Read Isaiah 43:1–3.

Do not fear, for I have redeemed you;

I have summoned you by name; you are mine.

When you pass through the waters,

I will be with you;

and when you pass through the rivers,

they will not sweep over you.

When you walk through the fire,

you will not be burned;

the flames will not set you ablaze.

For I am the LORD your God,

the Holy One of Israel, your Savior.

What does God promise His children in this Scripture passage?

- Wrap up your response time with prayer. Move from confession, to adoration, to thanksgiving, and end with your petitions (personal prayer needs).

YOUR GIG TRUST ADVENTURE JOURNAL

Spend a few moments contemplating and journaling about some of the scriptural truths that moved your heart as you read the devotions this week. Then write a prayer of response to God.

_____

_____

_____

_____

_____

_____

_____

_____

_____

_____

_____

_____

_____

_____

_____

_____

_____

_____

_____

_____

_____

_____

_____

_____

_____

_____

_____

Do not be afraid. Stand firm and you will see the deliverance the LORD will bring you today.... The LORD will fight for you; you need only to be still. (Exodus 14:13–14)

I Surrender!

Gwen Smith

Today's Truth

Whoever wants to embrace life and see the day fill up with good, here's what you do: Say nothing evil or hurtful; snub evil and cultivate good; run after peace for all you're worth. (1 Peter 3:10–11, MSG)

Friend to Friend

"I'm done with it! This battle just isn't worth fighting! I'm tired. It's hopeless." As I listened to my girlfriend verbally bleed from her wounded heart, I silently lifted up a prayer and asked God for wisdom. Her pain was real. Her troubles were not imaginary. She was desperate. She wanted a way out of the maze of disappointment and betrayal she had gotten lost in, out of the strong undertow of angst that had swept away her hope, out of the darkness that had covered her life and taken her captive.

No easy answers flooded my mind. I had no slick, three-point "sermonette" to offer her. I'm not a therapist. I don't even play one on TV. I'm just a Jesus-loving girl who tries to be there for her friends. So I didn't feel wise or brilliant that day as I gently, but confidently said, "I think the only way to win this battle is to surrender."

Surrender—not to the problem, but to the solution. Not to the conflict, but to the resolution. Both the solution and the resolution are found in the same nail-scarred hands. In order to win in any earthly struggle or relationship battle, we must put away the weapons of our wounding words and set aside the arsenal of our angry actions. Then with knees to the earth, we must raise a white flag in surrender...to the King.

What do we need to surrender? Our pride and expectations, our gripes and lamentations, our calculated manipulations, our righteous indignation, our doubts, and our frustrations.

Everything.

In order to live victoriously and win the battles we face in life, we've just got to surrender our flesh to the Spirit.

Summing up: Be agreeable, be sympathetic, be loving, be compassionate, be humble. That goes for all of you, no exceptions. No retaliation. No sharp-tongued sarcasm. Instead, bless—that's your job, to bless. You'll be a blessing and also get a blessing. (1 Peter 3:8–9, MSG)

On the battlefield of war, when we raise the white flag of surrender, we lose. But on the battlefield of life, when we surrender, we win—if, and only if, we surrender to God and not to our circumstances. We cannot control the variables beyond our own responses, but God will surely bless the woman who walks in obedience and who chooses to trust His sovereignty.

The text in 1 Peter goes on to say: "Whoever wants to embrace life and see the day fill up with good, here's what you do: Say nothing evil or hurtful; snub evil and cultivate good; run after peace for all you're worth" (verses 10–11 MSG).

We are able to run after peace and experience blessings of God in our day when we go before Him with a yielded heart. In a public address titled "Absolute Surrender," nineteenth-century pastor Andrew Murray said, "God is ready to assume full responsibility for the life wholly yielded to Him. The condition for obtaining God's full blessing is absolute surrender to Him."

What will that look like for you today? Are you ready to wave that white flag? Imagine what God will do in and through you each day as you choose to align your heart with His! Go there now. Be with the Strength-giver. Yield to the will of Him who loves you most. Blessings await you, friend.

Let's Pray

Lord, this is such a tough one! My life is complicated. It is very hard for me to relinquish control, yet I know that You are calling me to do just that. Help me to surrender my life into Your hands. Please dissolve my resentment, anger, fears, and frustrations. Help me to choose and trust Your ways, so that I can obtain the full blessings of absolute surrender. In Jesus's name, amen.

The Blanket

Sharon Jaynes

Today's Truth

In peace I will lie down and sleep, for you alone, LORD, make me dwell in safety. (Psalm 4:8)

Friend to Friend

"Where's my blanket?" my towheaded little Steven asked when we returned home from a trip.

"I think we left it at Grandma's house," I answered.

"We'll have to go back and get it," he decided.

"Honey, we can't. Grandma's house is too far away. You'll just have to do without it."

When my son, Steven, was four years old, he loved his blankie. It was yellow, fuzzy, and had a two-inch satin trim around the edge which he affectionately dubbed "his part." But this square of fluffy fleece was more than a blanket. This was Steven's security, comfort, and friend.

For four years, Steven's yellow blanket was his nighttime companion. Even during the day, I'd see him peek in his room to make

sure his friend was still waiting for his embrace. During his nap time, I'd watch as Steven clutched his yellow blanket, tucked it under his arm, and rubbed his fingers together over one particular satin covered corner.

"This is my part," he'd say with a smile.

And while Steven wasn't a continual thumbsucker, as soon as his hand grasped the blankie, especially "his part," the thumb automatically went in his mouth like a plug in a bottle. Those two companions—his blanket and his thumb—were all he needed to comfort his little-boy ills.

But there came a time in Steven's little-boy life when it was time to give up the blankie. "You're a big boy now," I explained, "and big boys don't suck their thumbs." But as soon as he caught a glimpse of the blanket, in went the thumb. After discovering the correlation and connection between the two, I knew what I had to do. During one of our visits to Grandma's, I made the tough decision and left it at her home.

Steven had a fitful night's sleep as he snuggled in his bed for the first time in his life without the comfort and security of his faithful friend clutched against his chest and his fingers rhythmically rubbing the magical part. But as the days and weeks passed, Steven's longing for the blanket subsided. Pretty soon he forgot about it altogether. And the thumb? While it stayed attached to his hand, it never went in his mouth again. He was turning into quite a little man.

Thinking back on Steven's dependence on his yellow blanket has caused me to consider the security blankets I have in my own life. No, I'm not talking about a literal blanket, of course, but about the vices I cling to for comfort. (It's funny. I stopped at the end of that sentence to take a sip of coffee. One of my vices, for sure.) Do I

depend on the approval of friends for security? Do I depend on a tidy appearance for acceptance? Do I cling to material objects for comfort? Do I grab a latte when I'm feeling blue?

God wants me to grow up. Sometimes that means putting away anything that I go to for comfort besides Him. That doesn't mean that I don't go to my husband or my friends when I need a hug or an encouraging word. It does mean that I determine not to depend on people, possessions, position, or performance for my ultimate security. People disappoint. God is always there.

One Easter season, a man was driving down the road with his granddaughter beside him in the front seat. As they passed by a neighborhood church, the little girl noticed three rugged crosses on the hillside. The middle cross was draped with a purple piece of cloth, symbolizing the resurrection of the King of kings.

"Look, Grandpa," the little girl remarked. "Jesus left His blankie."

Ah yes, Jesus left more than His blankie. He left us Himself— our only true source of security and comfort.

Is there something you've been clinging to for security? Perhaps God is calling you to let go and cling only to Him.

P.S. I have a secret. I still have Steve's yellow blanket. It's in a cedar chest with other treasures from his childhood. And I envision one day handing it to another little towheaded child…at least for a season.

Let's Pray

Dear God, You and You alone are my Rock, my Fortress, my Strong Tower, and my Hiding Place. Thank You for Your unfailing love. Forgive me when I run to another person besides You, when You are waiting for me to run to You. I love You. In Jesus's name, amen.

Springs of Living Water

Gwen Smith

Today's Truth

"Even now," declares the LORD, "return to me with all your heart, with fasting and weeping and mourning." Rend your heart and not your garments. Return to the LORD your God, for he is gracious and compassionate, slow to anger and abounding in love. (Joel 2:12–13)

Friend to Friend

Jeremiah was just a youngster when he came to know God and began to serve Him as a prophet. He endured year after year of hard times, frustrating people, and complicated disappointments. His message was one that called the people of Jerusalem—God's chosen people—to turn away from the idols they had been worshiping and back to the one true God.

Let me say it straight: God was miffed at the nation of Israel, and He sent Jeremiah to let them know that. And God had every reason to be angry! He had given the children of Abraham a sacred covenant, a promised future, delivery from oppression, and His

"tabernacled" presence, yet they turned their backs on Him. Continually. They doubted His exclusivity, and they set their attentions and affections on things other than God. They worshiped idols made of wood and stone, idols that were powerless and worthless. In Jeremiah 2:13, God said this of His people: "They have forsaken me, the spring of living water, and have dug their own cisterns, broken cisterns that cannot hold water."

Pastor Greg Laurie describes it this way: "A cistern is a large well or pool carved in a rock. A broken cistern has sprung a leak and can't hold water. God is saying, 'If you go out there to the world and drink from that well, it is not going to satisfy you.'"[3]

It sets my mind to wonder...

Why would anyone place her trust in the unstable, unpowerful, unfulfilling things of earth when she can place her trust in a stable, powerful, satisfying God? Seems like such a no-brainer—yet don't you and I do that all the time?

Sure we do.

We dig our own cisterns, broken cisterns, and expect them to satisfy our thirst and bring us contentment. We drink from the broken cisterns of materialism, position, wealth, popularity, stuff, relationships, rules, and religion. We have faulty expectations that our kids, spouses, and friends are meant to satisfy our heart-needs. The ultimate broken cistern, however, is our pursuit of purpose in life via things of this earth.

We were created to pursue God.

We were created to know God—to be satisfied in Him and Him alone.

---

3. Greg Laurie, "Friendship with the World," Greg Laurie Daily Devotions, November 28, 2007, Crosswalk.com.

We were created to worship Him and Him alone.

Oh, you and I are such a thirsty gaggle of girlfriends, aren't we? Even as believers, we deal with emptiness and bow to idols instead of God. We place our faith in the economy, in our financial situations, in our health, in our employment status, in our marital status, and our relationships. When one of these fails or fumbles, we fall apart—and no wonder! They are all broken cisterns and were never meant to be our source of hope or satisfaction!

Friend, we need to turn away from our broken cisterns and turn to the springs of living water. From stagnant waters to the Living Water. The Bible tells us that confession is the path to the spring of living water. When we eliminate the things that clutter our faith—the broken things we trust in—and place our faith in the resurrection power of Jesus Christ, God's heart swells with mercy, compassion, and grace toward us. He forgives us and strengthens us.

Who or what are you trusting in today?

Where are you soul-drinking from: broken cisterns or springs of living water?

When Jeremiah was preparing to take God's message of repentance to Jerusalem, God spoke confidence and promise to his shaking heart. Let these words speak confidence to your heart today, friend. God's promise to Jeremiah is valid for you and me whenever we turn away from the broken cisterns of this world and place our trust in Him. "'I am with you and will rescue you,' declares the LORD" (Jeremiah 1:19).

Jesus Christ is the Living Water our parched souls thirst for (see John 4:13–14). "Jesus stood and said in a loud voice, 'Let anyone who is thirsty come to me and drink. Whoever believes in me, as Scripture has said, rivers of living water will flow from within them'" (John 7:37–38).

Say with the psalmist: "As the deer pants for streams of water, so my soul pants for you, my God. My soul thirsts for God, for the living God" (Psalm 42:1–2).

Go to Him today. Confess. Believe. Drink. Be satisfied.

Let's Pray

Lord, I'm so thirsty for You! Please forgive me for the times that I have drunk from broken cisterns instead of from Your springs of living water. Thank You for Your compassionate grace and ever-flowing love. In a world that is constantly changing, I choose right now—once again—to place my trust in You, my unchanging God. In Jesus's name I pray, amen.

Everything Will Be Okay

Mary Southerland

Today's Truth

When you go through deep waters, I will be with you. When you go through rivers of difficulty, you will not drown. When you walk through the fire of oppression, you will not be burned up; the flames will not consume you. (Isaiah 43:2, NLT)

Friend to Friend

I am an avid reader. In fact, reading is one of my favorite ways to escape the sometimes chaotic pace of daily life. I also enjoy browsing through bookstores, especially the ones that provide cushy chairs where customers can sit quietly and read without being disturbed.

It is easy to tune out your surroundings and lose yourself in the pages of a good book. I was doing just that when I heard a familiar voice. Looking up, I spotted my friend Carol, who was asking an employee where she could find a suspense novel that had just been released. The young man quickly handed Carol the book from his personal stash behind the counter and went back to work. A smile

spread across Carol's face as she examined her new treasure while gently turning the book over in her hands and flipping through pages. Carol then did something I absolutely could not believe. She turned to the last several pages of the book and began reading.

It was time for an intervention. I was ready for the task.

I quickly put the book I had been reading back on the shelf. I needed to focus on the obvious needs of my friend. With a wave, I got Carol's attention and made my approach. "It is so good to see you," I said, giving her a gentle hug. "How have you been?" We spent a few minutes catching up on what was happening in our lives.

I could not help myself. "Are you buying that book?" I asked. It was an honest question because, for the life of me, I could not understand why anyone would want to buy a suspense novel when they already knew how it ended. Excitement danced in her eyes as she responded, "Yes, I am. I can't wait to read it. The ending is awesome!"

Now, I can understand reading the first few pages or scanning the table of contents before buying a book. I can even see the value of reading a few paragraphs here and there to get an idea of the story line. That makes sense to me. Carol's perspective did not. "Okay. I have to confess that I saw you reading the last few pages of the book. Why in the world did you read the ending? Won't that spoil the story for you?" I asked.

"Not at all," Carol quickly responded. "Before I buy a book, I always read the ending to make sure I really want that particular book." It was worse than I thought. Seeing the look of disbelief on my face, she laughed and admitted, "I know. It sounds crazy, but I have to know that everything turns out okay before I commit to reading the book."

The more I thought about Carol's words, the more I realized

that as followers of God, we have the assurance that everything really does turn out okay. Billy Graham once said, "I've read the last page of the Bible. It's all going to turn out all right."

When we focus only on what we can see and understand or explain, we will worry. Fear and doubt will become familiar companions if we live each day against the backdrop of this broken world. Our only hope is God, and He has already let us in on the ending of His story. In the meantime, it is not enough to just know *about* Him. We must *know Him.* A personal relationship with God through Jesus Christ assures us that no matter what the world throws our way, no matter what plot twists our lives take, it's all going to be okay.

Let's Pray

Father, I am tempted to worry about so many things. Our world is a mess! Forgive me for focusing on anything or anyone but You. Thank You for the Bible that equips and empowers me to live each day. Right now, I declare that You are my only Hope. Please help me to remember that You really are in control and You're making it all turn out all right. In Jesus's name, amen.

5

Jump In

Sharon Jaynes

Today's Truth

"Not by might nor by power, but by my Spirit," says the LORD Almighty. (Zechariah 4:6)

Friend to Friend

The bantering went back and forth for fifteen minutes until the little girl finally decided that she could trust her dad.

I was sitting on the balcony of a condominium at the beach listening to the excited squeals and splashes as children played in the swimming pool below. One particular little girl caught my attention. She appeared to be about six years old and wore bright yellow water wings that wrapped around her arms like blood pressure cuffs. She stood on the side of the pool nervously flapping her arms as her daddy stood poised in waist-deep water with his arms outstretched.

"Come on, honey. You can do it," he encouraged. "Go ahead and jump. I'm right here."

"But I'm scared," she whined as she flapped her arms.

"Don't be afraid. I'm right here," he assured her.

"But you might move. You might not catch me," she continued.

"I'm your daddy," he replied. "I'm not going to let anything happen to you." This bantering continued, and I marveled at the father's patience. Finally, after fifteen minutes of coaxing, the little girl jumped! Applause and laughter erupted from observers around the pool and on surrounding balconies! By the end of the morning, the little girl was making her way across the once seemingly treacherous waters like a carefree minnow.

Then God began to show me that sometimes I'm that little girl standing on the side of the pool.

"Come on! Jump in!" my heavenly Father calls.

"But I'm scared," I cry.

"Don't be afraid, my child. I'm right here," He assures me.

"But suppose I can't do it," I whine. "What if I sink? Suppose You move."

"I'm your heavenly Father," He replies. "I'm not going to let anything happen to you."

And the bottom line is this: it's all about trust. Do I trust God enough to jump into the seemingly treacherous waters of the unknown when He calls? Do I trust Him enough to obey Him in a sea of uncertainties?

All through the Bible we see people who were afraid to jump in. When God spoke to Moses through the burning bush and told him that he was going to lead the Israelites out of Egypt, Moses put up quite a fuss (see Exodus 3–4). "Who am I that I should go to Pharaoh and bring the Israelites out of Egypt?" Moses argued.

"I will be with you," God replied.

"Well, suppose I go to the Israelites and they ask me your name? Who shall I tell them sent me?"

"I AM WHO I AM," God replied. "Tell them I AM sent you."

"Well, what if they don't believe me or listen to me?" Moses

continued to argue. "I'm not a very good speaker. I'm not very eloquent. I have a speech impediment, for goodness' sake."

"I will help you speak and will teach you what to say," God replied yet again.

"Oh Lord, please send someone else to do it," Moses cried in one final plea.

Moses was just like that little girl standing on the side of the pool with her daddy coaxing her to jump in. Moses whined just as she had whined. And in both incidences, the father and the Father assured the reluctant children, "I'm right here. I'm not going to let anything happen to you. I will do it for you. I will help you. I will teach you."

And you know what? I'm not really any different than either of them. I'm sorry to say I've missed many opportunities because I chose to stand on the sidelines rather than dive into the divine appointments and wonderful opportunities He's laid out before me. Jesus said, "I have come that they [you] may have life, and have it to the full" (John 10:10). The Amplified Bible says it this way: "I came that they may have and enjoy life, and have it in abundance (to the full, till it overflows)." And through the years I've learned that the secret to discovering that abundant life is found when we jump in with both feet—but never let go of His hand.

What about you? Is God calling you to jump in? Is He coaxing you to step out of the safety of the sidelines and experience the incredible dreams He's dreamed for you? What's holding you back? Let's jump in!

Let's Pray

Heavenly Father, take away the fear that keeps me from stepping out in faith. Help me be a woman who accomplishes mighty feats for You while never letting go of Your hand. In Jesus's name, amen.

6

Now It's Your Turn

- This week we talked about placing our trust in things other than God. Things like security blankets and broken cisterns. We all struggle with this to some degree. How has this affected you in the past? How does it affect you in the present? And to go Dr. Phil on you: "How's that working for you?"

- As you grow in faith and get to know God's Word more, do you find that it is easier to place your trust in Him? Why or why not?

- In order to get to a place of deeper God-trust, we often need to come to a place of surrender. Take a moment to thoughtfully consider what barriers sometimes exist in your heart that keep you from being willing to surrender. (For example: pride, control, anger, fear...)

- What happens when you wave a white flag of soul-surrender and allow God to remove your heart-barriers?

- Can you think of a time recently when you were losing a situational battle because of your unwillingness to choose God's better way? What happened? (Don't gloss this up! Be real. We really need to have authentic introspection and conversations with our Girlfriends in God. Remember, if you are meeting with a GiG group, you don't *have to* share with one another, but we do ask

that you care for one another. All conversations are to be kept confidential.)

- How could that battle have been won by yielding to God in surrender? What could it possibly have looked like?

- List a few of the things that you fear.

  _____

  _____

  _____

- Read Isaiah 58:11: "The LORD will guide you always; he will satisfy your needs in a sun-scorched land and will strengthen your frame. You will be like a well-watered garden, like a spring whose waters never fail."

  Now place your name in the blanks. "The LORD will guide you always, _____; he will satisfy your needs in a sun-scorched land and will strengthen your frame. You, _____, will be like a well-watered garden, like a spring whose waters never fail."

- What does the Lord say He will do in the verses? Make personal statements by filling in the blanks below. Refer to Isaiah 58:11.

  God will _____ me always.

  God will _____ my

  _____ and

  _____ my frame.

  I will be like a _____ - _____ garden...whose waters will _____

  _____.

- Do you think that remembering God's faithful heart for His people will help wage war against the fears that long to consume and clutter your faith?
- Wrap up your response time with prayer. Move from confession, to adoration, to thanksgiving, and end with your petitions (personal prayer needs).

YOUR GIG TRUST ADVENTURE JOURNAL

Spend a few moments contemplating and journaling about some of the scriptural truths that moved your heart as you read the devotions this week. Then write a prayer of response to God.

_____

_____

_____

_____

_____

_____

_____

_____

_____

_____

_____

_____

_____

_____

_____

_____

_____

_____

_____

_____

_____

_____

_____

_____

_____

The LORD is my shepherd, I lack nothing. He makes me lie down in green pastures, he leads me beside quiet waters, he refreshes my soul. He guides me along the right paths for his name's sake. (Psalm 23:1–3)

The Tool of Discouragement

Mary Southerland

Today's Truth

Trust in the LORD with all your heart. (Proverbs 3:5)

Friend to Friend

It was advertised that the devil was putting his tools up for sale. When the day of the sale came, each tool was priced and laid out for public inspection. And what a collection it was. Hatred, envy, jealousy, deceit, pride, and lying...the inventory was treacherous. Off to one side was a harmless-looking tool priced higher than all the rest even though it was obviously more worn than any other tool the devil owned.

"What's the name of this tool?" asked one of the customers.

"That," the devil replied, "is discouragement."

The customer asked, "But why have you priced it so high?"

The devil smiled and explained, "Because discouragement is more useful to me than all the other tools. I can pry open and get inside a person's heart with that tool when I can't get near him with

any other. It's badly worn because I use it on almost everyone, since so few people know it belongs to me."

The valleys in life are lined with disappointment and discouragement. Some people seem to thrive on adversity, emerging from their valley with greater strength and deeper faith. Others stumble and fall, giving in to discouragement and dropping out of the race. The difference in outcome is determined by the way we choose to handle discouragement.

We must respond to each valley with trust and faith. One definition of the word *trust* means "to lie helpless, face down" and is the picture of a servant waiting for his master's command or a soldier yielding himself to a conquering general. *Heart* refers to "the center of one's being." In other words, to trust God completely means that from the very center of our being, from the very core of our existence, we trust Him, totally abandoning ourselves in childlike faith to Him and His plan. We come to God, holding nothing in our hands, with one word in our heart: *Whatever!* "Whatever You want me to do, Lord, I will do. Whatever You want me to say, Lord, I will say. Whatever You want me to think, Lord, I will think. Whatever path You have for me, Lord, I will walk."

If you are like me, you sometimes think you don't have enough faith. The amount of faith is not nearly as important as the right kind of faith—faith in God alone. Faith does not rest on what we have done, but on what Christ has already done on the cross and in our lives. Faith builds on the victories of yesterday to help us face the valleys of today and the mountains of tomorrow. Faith does not bypass pain. It does, however, empower us to deal with pain. Faith steps up to bat and invites the opponent to throw his best pitch. Sometimes faith strengthens us, and other times, surprises us. Great faith is

forged in the deepest valleys, beginning where our strength and power end.

I love the story of a missionary family, home on furlough and visiting friends. When it was time for dinner, the missionary mom called her kids in. When her son burst through the door, she took one look at his hands and said, "Son, go wash those hands. They are dirty and covered in germs." With a scowl on his face, the little boy headed to the sink muttering, "Germs and Jesus! Germs and Jesus! That's all I hear about and I've never seen either one!"

While we tend to say that seeing is believing, faith says that believing is seeing. Doubt creates mountains; faith moves them. Faith produces trust that shatters fear and leaves no room for discouragement.

Let's Pray

Father, I sometimes feel so discouraged. Life is just not turning out like I thought it would. I have had so many disappointments, and it seems like I face one valley after another. I need You and the hope that only You can give. Help me to trust You with all of my heart, not just part of it. Teach me how to walk by faith and not by sight. Today, I come to You with a yes in my heart for whatever You have planned for my life. In Jesus's name, amen.

2

Praise That Perseveres

Gwen Smith

Today's Truth

About midnight Paul and Silas were praying and singing hymns to God, and the other prisoners were listening to them. (Acts 16:25)

Friend to Friend

Andrea lives in Lake Mary, Florida, and is the proud momma of four beautiful girls. Two of her daughters are identical twins who have cerebral palsy and are severely disabled. Over the past fourteen years, Andrea and her husband have been wrung out with exhaustion. Her days are spent caring for the twins. And they are grueling days, often filled with many tears, outbursts of frustration, and bouts of anger. There have been times that she has felt abandoned by God. Andrea admits that, on many days, she has called out to God like the psalmist did: "Answer me when I call to you, my righteous God. Give me relief from my distress; have mercy on me and hear my prayer" (Psalm 4:1).

Through it all, however, Andrea has determined that she will praise God in spite of the daily complications. "I have always prayed for healing for my girls," she shares. "I believe our God could restore

my girls with one mere thought. I know that if He heals them, I will spend my life praising Him for that miracle and telling others of His goodness. Of course, although God *can* heal them, I've had to learn to spend my whole life praising Him simply because He is God—whether He heals the girls or not. I decided very early on that God is still God no matter what He allows in my life. I can trust Him even when I can't understand Him." She thoughtfully finished with, "It sounds easy, but it hasn't been."

Oh, how I can relate to honesty like that! How I'm drawn to this type of God-courage. Andrea's challenges are great, but she is determined to praise God anyway. When I hear stories like hers, my heart stretches toward trusting God. I hear and feel that the trials in her life have led her to a greater dependency on God and a deeper trust in His sovereignty. I'm reminded that in every situation, I come to a crossroads and have a choice: I can pout or I can praise. I can turn away from God because I don't understand, or I can turn toward Him in full assurance that His understanding is enough for the both of us—even if it hurts, even if anger lingers, even if doubt looms.

Have you been to these crossroads?

God shows us a powerful example of praise that perseveres in Acts 16. During the apostle Paul's second missionary journey, he and his ministry buddy Silas encountered a collision of faith and trouble while in Philippi. After Paul cast out a demon that was terrorizing a young slave girl, he and Silas were seized by disgruntled Roman citizens and dragged to the marketplace before the rulers. They were then wrongfully accused of public disruption. They were stripped, beaten, and unlawfully jailed without a trial. After the flogging, Paul and Silas were taken to the inner cell of the prison, normally reserved for the most dangerous offenders, and their feet were placed in stocks.

Though they had every reason to sit and stew about the injustice

of their situation, Paul and Silas chose to trust in God's plan and praise their Lord, Jesus Christ. Though they had open wounds and would have been in severe physical pain, Paul and Silas chose to glorify the name of God.

> After they had been severely flogged, they were thrown into prison, and the jailer was commanded to guard them carefully. When he received these orders, he put them in the inner cell and fastened their feet in the stocks. About midnight Paul and Silas were praying and singing hymns to God, and the other prisoners were listening to them. (Acts 16:23–25)

Then God shook the earth and the prison foundations and loosed the prisoners' chains. In horror, knowing he would be held responsible for the escape of the prisoners, the jailer raised his sword to kill himself—but Paul stopped him. He and Silas hadn't fled. They stood amid their dark circumstances and spoke and sang with confidence in their God.

As a result, several people, including the jailer and his family, came to believe in Jesus Christ:

> The jailer called for lights, rushed in and fell trembling before Paul and Silas. He then brought them out and asked, "Sirs, what must I do to be saved?"
>
> They replied, "Believe in the Lord Jesus, and you will be saved—you and your household." Then they spoke the word of the Lord to him and to all the others in his house. At that hour of the night the jailer took them and washed their wounds; then immediately he and all his household were

baptized. The jailer brought them into his house and set a meal before them; he was filled with joy because he had come to believe in God—he and his whole household. (verses 29–34)

Though we won't always rejoice in our circumstances, we are commanded to always rejoice in the Lord.

Rejoice in the Lord always. I will say it again: Rejoice!… Do not be anxious about anything, but in every situation, by prayer and petition, with thanksgiving, present your requests to God. And the peace of God, which transcends all understanding, will guard your hearts and your minds in Christ Jesus. (Philippians 4:4, 6–7)

Consider it pure joy, my brothers and sisters, whenever you face trials of many kinds, because you know that the testing of your faith produces perseverance" (James 1:2–3).

When we praise the Lord through and in spite of what we face, our praise becomes our deliverance through the trial.

We also have joy with our troubles, because we know that these troubles produce patience. And patience produces character, and character produces hope. And this hope will never disappoint us. (Romans 5:3–5, NCV).

No matter what difficult times we encounter, God is worthy of our praise. When we choose to praise, we choose to trust God. When we choose to trust God, people in the broken world around us lift their eyebrows in wonder—just like the Roman jailer. Sometimes a

sacrifice of praise is required. Offer it. We can and should choose to bless His name through the pain, which astonishingly can bring His joy into our hearts.

Let's Pray

Dear Lord, thank You for being trustworthy and praiseworthy! I ask that You will nudge me to trust You each time I approach the crossroads of faith and trouble. In spite of the burdens on my heart and challenges in my path right now, I praise Your name and celebrate that Your hope will never disappoint. In Jesus's name I pray, amen.

3

The Rose of Sharon

Sharon Jaynes

Today's Truth

No eye has seen, no ear has heard, and no mind has imagined what God has prepared for those who love him. (1 Corinthians 2:9, NLT)

Friend to Friend

My Bible lay open to the Song of Solomon, a very romantic book about the courtship, engagement, and eventual marriage between a man and a woman. Many compare it to the relationship of Jesus and His bride, the church. On this particular day, I chose to read the book as if I were reading a love story about Jesus pursuing me as His bride. This became even more real to me as I read the words in the first verse of chapter 2.

"I am a rose of Sharon," the woman said to her beloved.

What is your name? God seemed to ask.

"Lord, my name is Sharon," I whispered aloud.

Look it up, He prompted my heart.

I went to my Bible dictionary and looked up *Sharon*. Tears filled my eyes as I discovered that Sharon was a fertile valley near Mount Carmel. You see, after the birth of my first child, we struggled with

years of infertility. In my medical chart, somewhere among the diagnosis and prognosis of years of testing, is written the word *infertile*. And yet God was showing me that my name means "fertile valley." Then God began to show me that He had answered and surpassed my prayer for children, just not in the way I had imagined.

God fashioned women to bear children. Our wombs, breasts, hips, and hormones are uniquely designed for conceiving and giving birth. We have an inborn nature to nurture, and while some may give birth to their own flesh and blood in a delivery room and some do not, still we all can—and must—be fruitful and nurture those in our sphere of influence.

When God created Adam and Eve, He commanded them to "be fruitful and multiply, and fill the earth, and subdue it" (Genesis 1:28, NASB). In the New Testament, we see another kind of fruitfulness as Jesus sent out the disciples. "Therefore go and make disciples of all nations" (Matthew 28:19). He could have said, "Be fruitful and multiply," which is exactly what they did.

Though God has created women with a desire to nurture, I think that longing goes much deeper than just having children. Most of us long to invest our lives in something that matters. Usually that something is someone or many someones. The Bible calls that being fruitful. Jesus said, "I am the vine; you are the branches. If you remain in me and I in you, you will bear much fruit" (John 15:5). He also tells us that the true sign of a Christian is that they will bear fruit (see verse 8).

Sometimes, when our dreams are shattered, we have to let them die and allow God to birth other dreams in our lives. Like a seed that must be planted in the soil to grow, we must plant our disappointments in the soil of God's wisdom and wait for it to grow. A seed was never meant to remain a seed; it was meant to "be a fruit," to grow

into the God-ordained purpose hidden in its tiny hull. We grieve for a season, but in due time, purpose breaks from the buried seed, peeks through the soil of grief, and grows into what God intended all along. It is as if He were saying to us, "When you are letting go, remember that I am planting seeds of new life in you. Your grief is only for a season. My end is not death. It is always life. I am the Author of life."

This isn't only true for the dream of having children, but for all dreams we hold in our hearts.

God does not always give us the babies or the husband for which we prayed, but He will always give us access to everything we need to live an abundant life filled with purpose, passion, and His provision. When God says no, we can rest assured that He has a greater yes if we relinquish our shattered dreams to Him.

No, I don't have a house full of children with my blood coursing through their veins, but through ministry God has made me fertile by giving me more spiritual children than I ever could have imagined.

Someone asked me recently, "Would you rather have the house full of children or the spiritual children you have through ministry today?"

"I want exactly what God wants for my life—nothing more and nothing less," I answered, "because I know that whatever He has planned for my life is much greater than anything I could ever have imagined or conceived."

When we trust God and give Him our broken or unfulfilled dreams, He fashions them into a beautiful mosaic that is lovelier than anything we could have ever imagined. Is there a broken dream in your life today? Have you been holding on to the pieces? Open your hands. Lift them up. And give them to the Restorer of broken dreams today. You'll be surprised what a beautiful masterpiece will result.

Let's Pray

Heavenly Father, as Your daughter, I know You have a purpose and a plan for my life. Help me discover all You have prepared for me to do and give me the power and provision to do it. In Jesus's name, amen.

Praise God Anyway

Mary Southerland

Today's Truth

And the peace of God, which transcends all understanding, will guard your hearts and your minds in Christ Jesus. (Philippians 4:7)

Friend to Friend

I once saw a refrigerator magnet that read, "I know God promises to never give me more than I can handle, but sometimes I just wish He didn't trust me so much." Can you relate? When trials come and life is hard, we plead with God to deliver us *from* the problem when many times His plan is to deliver us *in* the problem. Praise does not depend upon an understanding of the circumstances or trial. Praise depends upon an understanding of who God really is and wants to be in our lives, and our willingness to trust Him.

As humans, we will never fully understand God—this side of heaven. God is holy and without blemish. God is all-powerful and omniscient. He is Creator of the universe, yet He lives in you and me at our invitation. He is the only true, living God!

We may understand some of His ways and comprehend the reasoning behind some of His plans. We may even come to the place of

knowing Him on an intimate level, but a full understanding of God is reserved for heaven. Until then, we walk by faith, not by sight. We praise Him in the darkness, knowing that the light is just ahead. We trust Him for things we cannot see, and we rest in Him in the valleys. Honestly, the thought of serving and relying on a God I can understand is not a reassuring thought.

Most people who know me well would describe me as a strong person, someone who can usually handle what life holds. I thought the same thing until I became a prisoner of the darkness as I battled severe clinical depression. It took me two long years to climb out of that pit, and not a day goes by that I am not reminded of that wonderful, horrible time. God used that first experience with the darkness in so many ways. He taught me new truths as He stripped away wrong attitudes and destructive thought patterns. I began to see myself as He sees me—loved, planned, and wanted. I began to trust Him as I never had before, and I found Him to be faithful—even when my faith was weak.

One of the many lessons I learned from my "pit experience" was that I cannot depend on my own strength or my unpredictable emotions. God often asked me to praise Him when, as far as I could tell, there wasn't a whole lot to praise Him for. I didn't *feel* like praising God because I didn't fully trust Him.

I began to understand that praise is not a feeling. Praise is a choice, a step of obedience taken without the assurance that circumstances will change or trials eliminated. Praise focuses on God, not the circumstances; praise fixes its gaze upon God's truth and His character instead of on the trial at hand or just ahead. That is why we can celebrate the battle before it begins. The outcome is neither our responsibility nor our goal. Praise begins and ends with faith in

the very nature, personality, and integrity of God…and that never changes.

No matter what lies ahead, God is faithful and you can trust Him. No matter how hot the fiery trial may be, God will deliver us in it or from it and will surely be with us as we go through it. No matter what people say or do, God loves and accepts us and promises that He will never leave us.

So praise God! Thank Him today for every victory that tomorrow holds. Celebrate—knowing that the battle belongs to God and, because of that single truth, victory is certain.

Let's Pray

Father, I praise You today for all that You have done in my life. You are faithful even when I am faithless. Your love pursues me even when I am unlovable. Your forgiveness covers my sin and frees me from its penalty. Lord, teach me to praise You. Help me to see and understand the power of praising You in my life. I want to bring You pleasure, Father. I praise You for Your love and faithfulness to me. Your presence in my life changes everything, empowering me to live each moment of every day, content in knowing You are in control. As I face today, Lord, remind me that no matter what happens, I can trust You. In Jesus's name, amen.

5

Unshakable Peace

Gwen Smith

Today's Truth

I have set the LORD continually before me; because He is at my right hand, I will not be shaken. (Psalm 16:8, NASB)

Friend to Friend

Susan lived "the good life." One filled with prosperity and love. For years, she and her husband owned a thriving business that allowed them and their children to be surrounded with beautiful material things. They had a glorious lake home, a lavish boat, and luxury cars—everything the world counts as gain.

In spite of their earthly wealth, when faced with the truth of the gospel, Susan and her husband realized that they were spiritually bankrupt and in desperate need of a Savior. Within months of each other, Susan and her husband both accepted Christ and began to thrive in newfound faith.

A few years into faith, Susan was squeezed by difficult circumstances. The family business had to close its doors, leaving many friends and employees jobless. Then the Internal Revenue Service audited her husband. Scary legal ramifications threatened to crush

them if large amounts of money were not paid to accommodate accounting debt. They lost everything. Financially ruined and emotionally stunned, Susan and her husband were forced to sell all that they owned.

Years later, they are still wading through the deep waters of financial strain. Their debts are far from being forgiven, and the economy has grown progressively dim. Through the turmoil, Susan has been learning to trust in God as her Provider. As she trusts Him, God faithfully fills her with supernatural peace, strength, and joy. She is experiencing God's provision through His Word, through His presence, and through her friends.

When her pantry has been empty, God knew. He sent friends to her home with bags of groceries and gift cards. When her soul has been discouraged, God knew. He sent reminders of His promises and love through Scripture and through the encouragement of godly women. Despite the fact that her bank account is still bare and the days are still complicated, Susan considers herself to be wealthier now than ever because she knows the soul-level, unshakable peace that is found in Jesus

As the time of His betrayal and crucifixion approached, Jesus told His disciples that though they would grieve His death, their grief would be turned to joy. He encouraged them to believe all that He said and gave them a compelling promise: "I have told you these things, so that in me you may have peace. In this world you will have trouble. But take heart! I have overcome the world" (John 16:33). He promised His bewildered disciples that, in Him, they would have peace in the midst of trouble. And how wonderful to know that His promise is valid for us, too.

No matter what you go through, you can experience unshakable peace and declare with the psalmist, "I will not be shaken" (Psalm

16:8)! God knows what you have been through and what you are going through. He promises peace to the believer through Jesus Christ.

Part of our unsettled nature is that we try to cling to the things of earth—to the "American way" of living—to the here and now. When we put our trust in things of this world, we give anxiety, fear, jealousy, discontentment, greed, and insecurity open access to our lives (see 1 Timothy 6:17–19).

Instead of finding ways to hold on to what you have, be encouraged today to let go. Let go of what doesn't matter. Even let go of those things that seem worth your worry:

> So do not worry, saying, "What shall we eat?" or "What shall
> we drink?" or "What shall we wear?" For the pagans run after
> all these things, and your heavenly Father knows that you need
> them. But seek first his kingdom and his righteousness, and all
> these things will be given to you as well. Therefore do not
> worry about tomorrow, for tomorrow will worry about itself.
> Each day has enough trouble of its own. (Matthew 6:31–34)

Seek God first, friend, above and before any earthly thing, large or small. Have faith that He will meet you at your need. God wants us to store up treasures where moth and rust will not destroy (see verses 19–20). He wants us to trust Him. When we do, He promises that we can live with an unshakable peace that passes understanding.

Let's Pray

Dear Lord, I need Your unshakable peace! Please forgive me for placing my trust and hope in things of this earth. As the psalmist David said, "Apart from you I have no good thing" (Psalm 16:2). Lead my soul to find rest in You and in Your perfect plan for my life. In Jesus's name, amen.

Now It's Your Turn

TIME FOR REFLECTION

- Read Hebrews 13:6: "We say with confidence, 'The Lord is my helper; I will not be afraid. What can mere mortals do to me?'"

    Do you see that we can choose to be unafraid and filled with God-confidence? God will help us! Is there a challenge in your life to which you can apply this scripture?

- Read 2 Corinthians 10:4–5 (NCV): "We fight with weapons that are different from those the world uses. Our weapons have power from God that can destroy the enemy's strong places. We destroy people's arguments and every proud thing that raises itself against the knowledge of God. We capture every thought and make it give up and obey Christ."

    Praise that perseveres begins with a determined mind, heart, and soul. The apostle Paul tells us to take control of our thought processes and train them to line up with God's will. When we learn to keep our gaze on God and our glance on circumstances, we will praise God. Where is your gaze today? Where is your glance?

- What steps can you take today that will help you remember to praise God when you come to the faith/trouble crossroads?

- Sometimes life does not turn out like we thought it would. Okay, not just sometimes, but most times. Is there any part of your life that seemed to take a bad turn, and then God showed you that it was indeed His perfect plan? What good did you see coming out of it?

- Is it possible that you are in a difficult position of your own making? Ask God to search your heart and reveal to you any ways that are contrary to His. Stop and pray right now.

- Do you really believe your life can bring God pleasure? Read Psalm 139. How does this psalm describe the way you look in God's eyes?

- Begin a Joy Journal by recording the daily blessings He gives you each day this week. Remember to add the "small" miracles as well as the "large" ones. At the end of the week, have a praise service—just you and God or with your GiG group. Thank Him for His presence and power at work in your life.

- Read Psalm 16. Underline your favorite verses and commit them to memory.

- Wrap up your response time with prayer. Move from confession, to adoration, to thanksgiving, and end with your petitions (personal prayer needs).

YOUR GiG TRUST ADVENTURE JOURNAL

Spend a few moments contemplating and journaling about some of the scriptural truths that moved your heart as you read the devotions this week. Then write a prayer of response to God.

_____

_____

_____

_____

_____

_____

_____

_____

_____

_____

_____

_____

_____

_____

_____

_____

_____

_____

_____

_____

_____

_____

Because your love is better than life, my lips will glorify you.
I will praise you as long as I live, and in your name I will lift
up my hands. (Psalm 63:3–4)

Look for the Pearls

Mary Southerland

Today's Truth

But he said to me, "My grace is sufficient for you, for my power is made perfect in weakness." Therefore I will boast all the more gladly about my weaknesses, so that Christ's power may rest on me. (2 Corinthians 12:9)

Friend to Friend

Life can be so irritating. More often than not, it's the little things that annoy me the most: the lost set of keys, the misplaced cell phone, the icemaker that refuses to do its job on a hot summer day, the empty tea pitcher stuck back in the refrigerator. I am convinced that these tiny irritations are a tool in the hands of a loving Father who uses them as "heavenly sandpaper" to rub off some of our rough edges.

I was invited to speak for a women's conference based on the theme "Pearls of Wisdom." When I arrived at the conference center, I was greeted by women wearing pearl necklaces, pearl bracelets, pearl pins, hats covered in multicolored pearls… You name it, and

they wore it if it had pearls. Each table was beautifully decorated with treasure chests overflowing with strands of pearls. Oyster shells held candy mints that looked like pearls, and each name tag was decorated with a single pearl. It was amazing!

I was warmly welcomed and then promptly introduced to the event director and leadership team who were excited and ready to go—except for one problem. I was "pearl-less." I was quickly told that the speaker *had* to wear pearls of some kind. I did not have any pearls, but this creative group of ladies was not easily deterred. Before I knew it, I was wearing a stunning pearl necklace—and the pearls were the real deal. I could just see that necklace breaking while I was speaking, but before I could utter one word of protest, the owner of the necklace said, "Don't worry! You can just give it back to me at the end of the conference." And off we went!

I am what you might call an "active" speaker in that I cannot stand still and talk at the same time. I get excited, pace the stage, wave my arms and can literally work up quite a sweat. The Pearls of Wisdom conference was no exception. In fact, it was a blistering summer day and the air conditioning was having trouble keeping up with the size of the crowd. By the time I finished speaking, I was indeed "glowing." When we were dismissed for the day, women waited in line to talk, ask for prayer, or share a new truth God had given them. I forgot all about the pearl necklace until its owner quietly slipped up beside me and said, "I have to leave and need to retrieve my necklace." As she began to undo the necklace clasp, I apologized for perspiring all over her beautiful pearls. She laughed and said, "Actually, it is good for them. Human perspiration helps the pearls keep their luster."

I am constantly amazed at the profound truths God has tucked

into the simple things of life. Pearls are formed when a piece of grit, sand, or shell is trapped inside an oyster. The oyster protects itself from irritation by secreting a nacreous liquid that surrounds the irritant until it eventually becomes a pearl. In other words, what begins as an annoying irritant eventually becomes a valuable treasure. The same is true in life.

I tend to look for the nearest exit when sand enters the oyster of my life. Avoiding complicated circumstances tends to be one of my most common goals. Can you relate? What we really need to do is cultivate an attitude of unshakable confidence in God and keep a "but God" promise in our heart:

"My husband has lost his job, *but God* will provide."

"The doctors have said there is no hope, *but God* is the Great Physician."

"I don't know what to do, *but God* will show me the way."

Looking back, I can honestly say that I have found the greatest treasures during the darkest times. A battle with clinical depression stripped away years of fear and doubt, leaving me with a new identity in Christ and a ministry I never thought possible. The inability to have biological children made it possible to adopt our two children, giving my husband and me a gift beyond measure. Over the years, weaknesses have given way to strengths and failures have led to successes and God has used it all for His glory and my good.

We live in uncertain times, but in God's economy, a mess is the perfect setting for a miracle, girlfriend. A sliver of hope and a seed of victory are buried at the center of every problem. God has gone before you. He has already been where you are going, and in every trial or difficult moment of life, God has buried a treasure. When the tough times come, just look for the pearls.

Let's Pray

Father, I am so sorry for the way I complain about my circumstances. Please forgive me for my bad attitude when things don't go my way. I want to see Your hand in every part of every day, good or bad. Help me learn how to face every storm with confidence and trust in You. In Jesus's name, amen.

Comfort-Able

Sharon Jaynes

Today's Truth

In this you greatly rejoice, though now for a little while you may have had to suffer grief in all kinds of trials. These have come so that the proven genuineness of your faith—of greater worth than gold, which perishes even though refined by fire—may result in praise, glory and honor when Jesus Christ is revealed. (1 Peter 1:6–7)

Friend to Friend

My son and I sat on the floor in his room playing rummy. We had just a few minutes before rushing off to register him for his summer swim class, but we wanted to get in one more round of play. This summer was proving to be the best ever. Our golden retriever, Ginger, had just delivered seven adorable puppies, Steven was enjoying his sixth summer of life, and after four years of the heartache of negative pregnancy tests, God had surprised us with a new life growing inside my womb.

But as Steven and I sat on the floor, I felt a warm, sticky sensation run down my leg. A trip to the bathroom confirmed my greatest

fear. Later that afternoon, our baby died and is now waiting for us in heaven.

What began as a summer full of life and joy quickly turned into a season of great loss and sadness. I mourned for that child for whom I had prayed, and I felt the ache of empty arms. Someone once said, "I never knew I could miss someone I had never met." But, oh, how I missed her. We never knew for sure, but in my heart, I felt that the baby had been a little girl.

During those summer months, I went through the grieving process step by step. I'll admit that I was angry at God for "taunting" me with this gift of a child and then taking her away. But through the months and years that followed, God taught me many lessons about myself, about Him, and about trusting in His unfailing love.

I believe that when we go through a trial that wounds us deeply, God can use it to teach us valuable lessons. Some of those lessons are a deeper understanding of who God is, of who we are, and of what we truly believe. Our faith grows in the petri dish of struggles in the laboratory of life. One of my most valuable lessons, through all my wounds and scars, was a decision to stop saying, "Why me?" and to begin saying, "What now?" But the lesson that continues reverberating like a gentle thunder is the truth of God's unfailing love.

During the months that followed the loss of our child, I struggled with God. Just as Jacob wrestled with God through his dark night of the soul, I wrestled as well. *How could He love me and allow this to happen? Why would God withhold my dream? Is He able? Is He kind? Is He really there?*

It was a dry summer…in my heart and soul. No one could help me, comfort me, or lift me out of my despair. And while I didn't want to talk to God, He never left my side. Patiently, He waited for

me to cry out to Him, to say, "I will trust You even though I do not understand."

One of the nuggets of gold I discovered in this dark situation is the ability to help other women who are experiencing loss in their own lives. I love this verse: "Praise be to the God and Father of our Lord Jesus Christ, the Father of compassion and the God of all comfort, who comforts us in all our troubles, *so that* we can comfort those in any trouble with the comfort we ourselves receive from God" (2 Corinthians 1:3–4). In other words, God doesn't comfort us to make us comfortable. God comforts us to make us comfort-able, able to comfort others.

While there is nothing wrong with trying to understand why the wounds of life occur, the Bible clearly tells us not to depend on or lean on our own ability to answer the tough question "Why?" "Trust in the LORD with all your heart," the writer of Proverbs tells us, "and lean not on your own understanding" (3:5). Don't depend on your own mind to figure out life. In *When God Doesn't Make Sense,* Dr. James Dobson says, "Trying to analyze His [God's] omnipotence is like an amoeba attempting to comprehend the behavior of man."[4] It is simply not possible. And that brings us to what trust is really all about. It is based on our confidence in the infinite God whose ways our finite human minds cannot understand. If we could understand Him and His ways completely, then there would be no need for trust at all. True trust is trusting God in the dark.

But there is one thing we can be sure of. "All the ways of the LORD are loving and faithful" (Psalm 25:10) whether we understand them or not.

---

4. James Dobson, *When God Doesn't Make Sense* (Wheaton, Ill: Tyndale House, 1993), 8.

Have there been difficult situations in your life that you still don't understand? Are you willing to let them go and trust that God has a purpose and a plan? Patiently, He is waiting for us to cry out to Him…to say, "I will trust you even though I do not understand."

Let's Pray

Dear Father, I'll admit there are certain aspects and events in my life that I do not understand. Today, I am choosing to stop saying, "Why me?" and to begin asking, "What now?" You are the Potter and I am the clay. Mold me and shape me to become the vessel that best serves Your precious purposes. In Jesus's name, amen.

Practice Makes Progress

Gwen Smith

Today's Truth

In the night, Lord, I remember your name, that I may keep your law. This has been my practice: I obey your precepts. You are my portion, Lord; I have promised to obey your words. (Psalm 119:55–57)

Friend to Friend

I'm a sporty girl—always have been. I love to power walk and keep fit. I grew up playing lots of different athletic games—from basketball to softball—but volleyball has always been my sport of choice. I just love the game. I love the quick pace, the demands on strength and agility, and the team component of the matches.

In college, I had the opportunity to play volleyball, and now that I'm a mom I coach my daughter's team. I've been around this game for more than twenty-five years, and I've spent more time on the court, on the sand, and on the grass playing and practicing than

most people ever will. You'd think that after all the hours invested, I'd have the game perfected by now, right? Not hardly.

There are still times when I shank a pass—when the ball flies off my arms wildly in the wrong direction. I still have spike attempts that send the ball into the net instead of over the net. There are still times when I miss a serve. Each mistake frustrates me. Seriously. I'm competitive and I hate to lose. I hate to make mistakes, and I almost always think I should've played better than I actually did. No matter how much I've grown as a player since I first picked up a volleyball, I've come to realize that when I step on the court, there will always be frustrating shanked passes and there will always be opportunities for me to grow and progress in my skills. Simple as that.

And you know what? I've found the same to be true in my prayer life.

Do you remember that old saying, "Practice makes perfect"? Well, I think it's a bunch of beans! I recently heard a phrase that better represents the reality of growth and development: practice makes *progress*. Whether we're talking about our development as athletes, as students, as wives, as employees, or simply as women of faith—specifically, as women of prayer—we are all purposed for growth until we die.

The truth that the apostle Paul wrote about in Romans 7 still remains: we don't do what we should do and we do what we shouldn't. Whew! I can so relate. Prayer, I'm afraid, is one of the "don't dos" for many of us. We all seem to know how important it is to trust God with our burdens, but many of us neglect this important discipline. Do you ever go to the phone before you go to the throne? Yeah, me too. There are times when I fail to trust God with my prayers. And though I've been faith-walking with Him a long time, there are still

a million ways that I need to grow. There will always be ways for us to grow and there will always be mistakes for us to work through.

Our relationship with God will grow as we continually turn to Him in prayer. Similarly, our trust in God grows as our relationship with Him grows. "I no longer call you servants, because a servant does not know his master's business. Instead, I have called you friends, for everything that I learned from my Father I have made known to you" (John 15:15). Jesus counts us as His "friends." How many of us would talk to our close friends as infrequently as we talk to Jesus, our Creator and Redeemer?

Of course, it's not like we can ignore the world around us and pray 24/7. Right? We are still going to go to work, play, and spend time with friends and family, but in the midst of it all, Scripture instructs us to "rejoice always, pray without ceasing, give thanks in all circumstances; for this is the will of God in Christ Jesus for you" (1 Thessalonians 5:16–18, ESV). Our practice of this continual prayer life will increase our progress in faith and in trusting God. This can translate into prayers of thankfulness and petition during our power walks, our time in the carpool line, while we wash our laundry, and when we take our lunch breaks. We can redeem these times by thanking God for and praying for our children, our careers, our futures, our marriages, our trials, and our challenges. When we "do life" with God—when we exercise this spiritual discipline of continuous prayer—our faith grows. It helps us to trust Him more.

Even Jesus, the only perfect Man, turned to our Father continually. He gave thanks for food when He prayed over the loaves and fishes that became a miracle (Matthew 14:16–21). He took His sorrows to God in the garden before His execution on the cross (Matthew 26:39). He prayed for His friends (John 17:6–19), for Himself

(verses 1–5), and for future believers (verses 20–26). Jesus also modeled how we should pray (Matthew 6:5–15), and He taught about prayer (Luke 11:1–13). If Jesus, the God of the Universe, saw prayer as such an important part of the Christian life, why do we sometimes overlook the importance of it? We need to make time to turn to Him and trust Him with our daily concerns, big and small.

A strong volleyball team is one where teammates rely on one another in the game. As Christians, we have the advantage. We have God on our team. And with God on our team, we cannot fail. Seriously. If God is for us, who can stand against us? We just need to talk to Him and trust Him rather than trying to play the game of life on our own. We have to remember that practice makes progress! We will learn to trust as we practice trusting the Lord through prayer.

Let's Pray

Dear God, that You would choose to call me friend is simply amazing! Thank You that though I'm not perfect, Your grace allows me to progress in faith! Please forgive me for the times when I go about my day and "do life" without You. Help me to continuously pray and to trust You with my burdens. In Jesus's name I pray, amen.

Strong in the Broken Places

Mary Southerland

Today's Truth

I will give you hidden treasures, riches stored in secret places, so that you may know that I am the LORD, the God of Israel, who summons you by name. (Isaiah 45:3)

Friend to Friend

I love a great movie. To me, a movie is only great—no matter what any movie critic says or how many stars the film is granted—when good wins over evil, the right guy gets the girl, nobody gets hurt and everyone lives happily ever after. A bit naive, I know, but I have decided that there is enough harsh reality traipsing through my daily life without paying to see more on a movie screen. When I sit down in that cushy theater seat, popcorn and soda in hand, I want happy endings.

With these criteria in mind, I went to see the movie *Sea Biscuit*. God has a way of wrapping remarkable truths in unremarkable circumstances.

There I was, munching and sipping away, minding my own business and enjoying my brief respite from the real world, when God's words echoed through the movie theater and slammed into my soul.

"You don't throw a whole life away just because it's banged up a little," the horse trainer explained. I was done. I thoroughly enjoyed the rest of the movie, but those simple words seemed to be written just for me, and lingered long after the credits scrolled across the movie screen.

We are all "banged up a little" by life. I know what it feels like to be broken and in pain. And I do not like it—a fact that seems meaningless when it comes to facing and dealing with tough experiences. The hits just keep coming.

I have a choice to make. I can surrender to the darkness and create an identity that feels at home in a pit, or I can embrace the pain and learn from it. I can settle for a life defined by pain, or I can harness the power of my pain and use it for good. I can try to ignore the pain and hope it all goes away, or I can face it and let God heal the broken places.

After our son broke a bone in his foot during a high school football game, we took him to an orthopedic surgeon who explained exactly what he would do during surgery. "I will remove any scar tissue that has formed around the break and insert a metal screw to connect the broken bones." As he spoke, I was comforted by my mind's depiction of a shiny, thin, and smooth metal screw resting gently in my son's foot. Ignorance really can be bliss.

The surgery went well. During a follow-up visit, the doctor walked in, smiling and waving an x-ray in his hand. "Your foot is healing beautifully," he announced with great pride. Curious, I

asked if we could see the x-ray. When he slapped it up against the light board, I was horrified to see a thick, long metal bolt. In fact, on closer examination, I was certain the beginnings of rust could be seen on that barbaric screw jammed into my precious son's bone.

The doctor quickly assured me that everything was fine. I was far from convinced and had a few questions that needed answering—immediately: "Is that screw supposed to look like that, or did you put the wrong screw in my son's foot? Will he be able to play football? Will his foot hurt when it rains? Will that enormous screw set off airport security detectors? Will Jered's foot ever be as strong as it was before the surgery?"

The doctor listened patiently, smiled, and finally said, "Well, now that you mention it, I need to be honest and tell you that Jered's foot will *not* be as strong as it was before." The evil doctor then grinned and said, "It will actually be stronger."

I find it interesting that, all through life, the greatest strength is forged in broken places. In *A Farewell to Arms,* Ernest Hemingway wrote, "The world breaks everyone and many are strong at the broken places." God spoke through the prophet Isaiah: "I will give you hidden treasures, riches stored in secret places, so that you may know that I am the Lord, the God of Israel, who summons you by name" (Isaiah 45:3).

Wow! The truth of this verse rocks my world. God has gone before us and buried a treasure in every problem and stored rich truths in every minute of darkness we will face. The only way we can discover that treasure is to embrace the problem as an opportunity to trust God and uncover a new seed of victory. Some things cannot be learned in the light—they are treasures of the darkness.

Let's Pray

Father, my heart is broken, and I don't understand what You are doing in my life. The darkness is very real, and filled with more questions than answers. And I don't like it! But I love You, Lord, so I choose trust over fear and faith over doubt. Lord, please fill each broken place in my heart with Your peace and love. Today, I choose You. In Jesus's name, amen.

My Only Son

Sharon Jaynes

Today's Truth

He who did not spare his own Son, but gave him up for us all—how will he not also…graciously give us all things? (Romans 8:32)

Friend to Friend

I stood at Steven's bedroom door, watching this now seventeen-year-old son sleep in a tangle of sheets and limbs. He was six feet tall, he needed a shave, and he sported a mass of thick, shaggy brown hair. I thought about how much I loved this boy.

When Steven was born, we had no idea we would be raising him as an only child. Years of infertility struggles and the loss of our second child had left us with a hollow echo of the heart we feared would never be filled. And yet, when I looked at this sleeping man-child, love filled every nook and cranny of my heart till I thought it would burst. Still, there was always the wondering what life would have been like had more Jaynes children filled the rooms, scattered their toys, and left handprints on the walls.

"Lord," I prayed, "You know how much I love children and how I always longed to be a mom to a houseful of children. I know Your

ways are higher than our ways and that You are my heavenly Father who knows what's best for me. But God, could You show me a purpose behind the pain of those difficult years of longing? You certainly don't owe me an explanation, but I'd love to have a bit of encouragement today."

Standing in the doorway, watching the rhythmic rise and fall of Steven's steady breathing, God's Word washed over me.

For God so loved the world that he gave his one and only Son, that whoever believes in him shall not perish but have eternal life (John 3:16).

"Is that You, Lord?" I asked. "Is that my nugget of gold?"

For God so loved the world that he gave his one and only Son, that whoever believes in him shall not perish but have eternal life.

The words washed over me again like a spring rain on parched ground, and my breath caught. It was as if the Holy Spirit illuminated Steven like a lone actor on the stage. Steven…my one and only son. For the first time in my life, I truly grasped the height, the depth, and the breadth of those familiar words. Jesus…God's one and only Son.

Yes, I have a one and only son as well. I love many people in this world, but none enough to sacrifice my only son. And yet God loved *me* that much. He loved *you* that much. He loved us enough to sacrifice His one and only Son in order to make eternal life with Him possible.

All through those years of infertility and loss, Satan, the Enemy, taunted me with words of doubt. *God doesn't love you,* he'd say. *If He loved you, He'd give you what you asked for. He doesn't love you. You can't trust Him with your heart.*

And yet, at that moment when I stood in Steven's doorway, I realized just how much God *did* love me. He had shone the light of His love on the Enemy's lie and revealed the truth.

With tears spilling down my cheeks, I thanked God for helping me understand His great love—for giving me a living, breathing daily reminder of that love every time I looked at my boy. If that was the only purpose behind the years of infertility and loss of a child, then that was enough.

The Bible says, "And we know that in all things God works for the good of those who love him, who have been called according to his purpose" (Romans 8:28). What does God really mean by "all things"? Most likely He means all things—the good, the bad, and the ugly. I believe that in every dark circumstance of life, there is a nugget of gold or a hidden treasure just waiting to be discovered. However, for that to happen, we must look beyond the dirt, push it aside, and search beneath the surface.

Is it easy? No. Is it messy? Usually. Is it worth it? Always.

Has there been a trial or loss in your life? If so, I wonder if God has a valuable treasure hidden beneath the surface of the pain, just waiting to be discovered. Do you trust Him enough to push the dirt aside and see?

Let's Pray

Heavenly Father, thank You for loving me so much that You gave Your only Son so that I could receive eternal life the moment I believed in Him. In Jesus's name, amen.

Now It's Your Turn

TIME FOR REFLECTION

- No doubt about it—life can be tough. What is your normal response to a problem or trial? And how is that working for you?
- When hard times come, we need to look for God instead of the nearest exit. In fact, James says we should throw a party ("consider it pure joy" [1:2]) and celebrate the trials in our lives. Why? Because every trial is also an opportunity for God to transform tragedy into triumph—if we are willing to trust Him.
- During Sharon's years of infertility and the loss of a child, she struggled with feelings of insecurity and fear and found it hard to believe that God really did love her. Have you ever felt that way when you were going through a difficult time?
- Read Psalm 40:1–3, and record these verses in your journal.

I waited patiently for the LORD;
    he turned to me and heard my cry.
He lifted me out of the slimy pit,
    out of the mud and mire;

he set my feet on a rock
>and gave me a firm place to stand.

He put a new song in my mouth,
>a hymn of praise to our God.

>Go back and circle the action words in these verses.
>Which ones apply to you? Which ones apply to
>God? What does this passage tell you about
>God's faithfulness to us even when our faith is
>small?

- Every problem in our lives can be met with the promises of God. "The LORD is my strength, my shield from every danger. I trust in him with all my heart. He helps me, and my heart is filled with joy" (Psalm 28:7, NLT 1996 edition).

    Fill in the blanks with the problems you are facing .
    Then add a promise God has for each one. For
    example: "I am afraid…but God will take care
    of me."
    I am _____…but God will

    _____.

    I am _____…but God will

    _____.

    I am _____…but God will

    _____.

- Wrap up your response time with prayer. Move from confession, to adoration, to thanksgiving, and end with your petitions (personal prayer needs).

Your GiG Trust Adventure Journal

Spend a few moments contemplating and journaling about some of the scriptural truths that moved your heart as you read the devotions this week. Then write a prayer of response to God.

_____

_____

_____

_____

_____

_____

_____

_____

_____

_____

_____

_____

_____

_____

_____

_____

Consider it pure joy, my brothers and sisters, whenever you face trials of many kinds, because you know that the testing of your faith produces perseverance. Let perseverance finish its work so that you may be mature and complete, not lacking anything. (James 1:2–4)

Help Me, Lord!

Sharon Jaynes

Today's Truth

But I trust in you, LORD; I say, "You are my God."… Let your face shine on your servant; save me in your unfailing love. (Psalm 31:14, 16)

Friend to Friend

"Get it out! Get it out!" Steven cried as he held his hand over his eye. He was eight years old at the time and had been playing on the playground when a piece of bark flew into his eye.

"Get it out!" he cried as he ran into the house.

"Son, you're going to have to take your hand away if you want me to remove the bark."

"No, don't touch it," he cried. "It'll hurt!"

"It already hurts," I replied. "Now take your hand away so I can get it out."

Steven kept his hand over the eye and wouldn't let me touch it. He went back and forth between "Get it out!" and "Don't touch it!" for about forty-five minutes. Finally the pain overcame his fear, and

he decided to trust me. Yes, it took forty-five minutes for me to convince him to remove his hand and twenty seconds for me to remove the piece of bark in his eye.

As he ran back out into the yard to play, I saw myself in Steven's struggle. So many times I cry out to God, "Get it out! Get it out!" I desperately need God to take care of a problem that is causing me pain and yet at the same time I hold on to it so tightly He can't. What I saw in this earthly struggle between parent and child was merely a reflection of the heavenly struggle God must have with me.

Trust always precedes a miracle.

- Noah trusted in God's command to build an ark, even though it had never rained on the earth before.
- Abraham trusted in God's command to leave his homeland, even though God didn't tell him where He was sending him.
- Joshua and Caleb trusted God's command to march into the Promised Land, even though it was filled with giants and mighty warriors.
- Joshua trusted in God's command to march around Jericho seven times for seven days blowing trumpets, even though it seemed like a strange battle plan.
- Esther trusted in God's leading to go before the king and plead for the lives of her people, even though it could have meant her death.
- Samuel trusted in God's command to anoint a little shepherd boy named David as the next king of Israel, even though David was only a teen.
- Peter trusted in Jesus's instruction to throw his net out into the lake one more time, even though he had been fishing all night and caught nothing.

Trust always precedes the miracle. I can almost hear God now: *Sharon, you're going to have to take your hand away if you want Me to take care of the problem. You are going to have to trust Me if you want to see the miracle.*

Ponder the words in this poem by an unknown author:

Just as my child brings his broken toys with tears for me
   to mend,
I took my broken dreams to God, because He was my friend.
But then instead of leaving Him in peace to work alone,
I hung around and tried to help with ways that were my own.
At last I snatched them back and cried, "How could you be
   so slow?"
"What could I do, my child?" He said. "You never would let go."

It can be hard to open our tightly held fists and give God the pieces of our broken lives. I think of the story I heard about a little boy, much like my own, who had his hand caught in a valuable vase. His parents tried and tried to get his hand free, but after many attempts, it became apparent they were going to have to shatter the beautiful porcelain in order to set him free. But before the hammer came down, his father tried one more time.

"Son," he said, "I want you to open your fingers and then bring them together at the fingertips. Then try one more time to slip your hand out of the vase."

"I can't do that, Daddy," the little boy explained, "because if I do, I'll drop my penny."

Oh, dear friend, God wants to restore our broken dreams and wounded hearts. But that means we have to trust God and open our tightly clenched fist and let go of the pennies of life.

Let's Pray

Heavenly Father, I can be so stubborn. Today, I'm letting go of my struggles and placing them into Your capable and caring hands. I trust You. Now, help me not to take them back. In Jesus's name, amen.

No Safety Net

Mary Southerland

Today's Truth

The LORD answered him, "I will be with you. It will seem as if the Midianites you are fighting are only one man." (Judges 6:16, NCV).

Friend to Friend

I was born to be an elementary school teacher—period. So when a total stranger tapped me on the shoulder and said, "While you were singing, God told me that you are supposed to be my music and youth assistant this summer," I felt sorry for him. He obviously needed to have his hearing checked.

I had just graduated from college with a degree in elementary education. A good friend was leading worship for a local church and had asked me to sing a solo. That's all—or so I thought—until *my* good friend introduced me to *his* good friend, the hard-of-hearing stranger, and said, "You should at least pray about his offer." I did. And here I am, thirty years later, an unlikely servant who lives in constant amazement at God's plan for her life.

The Bible is filled with people who were unlikely servants. Weak

and fearful, they fought against the call of God, offering excuses and pleading for exemption, just as we do today. Gideon was such a man.

> One day the angel of GOD came and sat down under the oak in Ophrah that belonged to Joash the Abiezrite, whose son Gideon was threshing wheat in the winepress, out of sight of the Midianites. The angel of GOD appeared to him and said, "GOD is with you, O mighty warrior!"
>
> Gideon replied, "With *me,* my master? If GOD is with us, why has all this happened to us? Where are all the miracle-wonders our parents and grandparents told us about…? The fact is, GOD has nothing to do with us—he has turned us over to Midian."
>
> But GOD faced him directly: "Go in this strength that is yours. Save Israel from Midian. Haven't I just sent you?"
>
> Gideon said to him, "*Me,* my master? How and with what could I ever save Israel? Look at me. My clan's the weakest in Manasseh and I'm the runt of the litter."
>
> GOD said to him, "I'll be with you. Believe me, you'll defeat Midian as one man." (Judges 6:11–16, MSG)

Gideon was a farmer, a family man just trying to put food on the table. He felt inadequate to carry out God's plan for his life. But God saw what Gideon could be, not just what he was. The fact that the angel called Gideon a "mighty warrior" is funny. Gideon didn't look or act the part. Normally, wheat was threshed in an open area on a threshing floor. But Gideon did his work in a winepress, hiding from the Midianites. I don't blame him. The Midianites were basically terrorists—a large and powerful army of nomadic invaders. God

wanted Gideon to defeat them and set the Israelites free. I can imagine the look on Gideon's face and the sheer panic in his heart when God told him the plan.

Are you talking to me?

You want me to do what? Funny!

I am weak. I come from the wrong side of the Manasseh tracks. People like me don't save nations and defeat armies.

I don't think Gideon was being humble. I think he was terrified and convinced that he was totally unqualified for the job God was asking him to do. I know that feeling. I tend to use my weaknesses as excuses for disobedience instead of accepting them for what they really are: opportunities for God to show up and show off in my life. But just as God was with the flawed Gideon, He is with us.

God's commitment *to* Gideon reaffirmed His presence *with* Gideon and the ease with which Gideon would defeat the Midianites. The literal translation is "as if they were but one man." God was telling Gideon that the victory would be so easy that it would seem like he was facing one man instead of an army of fierce invaders.

Gideon's attitude was still lousy; he blamed God for getting the Israelites into their current mess, and he voiced major doubts about God's willingness or desire to save them. Gideon sputtered every excuse imaginable, venting his confusion while questioning the validity of God's choice. But God insisted that Gideon was the man for the job.

Actually, making excuses is pointless because God is completely aware of who we are and what we can and cannot do. He always equips and empowers us to obey Him. The Lord told Gideon to "go in the strength you have." God was asking Gideon to step out in faith, knowing that his meager strength would not be enough. But

that's what faith is all about—being willing to step out in mid-air, no safety net in sight, trusting God to be there at the point of our greatest need.

I have a love/hate relationship with the movie *Indiana Jones and the Last Crusade*. The hero, Indiana Jones, is constantly hovering above some bottomless pit or dodging bullets, flying knives, or sinister enemies who are trying to kill him so he can't complete his mission. At one point, Indiana is on the run and comes to a chasm he must cross in order to obtain the Holy Grail. No bridge. No net. No ropes or hat tricks—just air, and nothing but air.

At this point in the movie, I find myself looking for a tangible resolution to Indiana's predicament—maybe a hidden elevator or an alternate route. You know, something he could touch and see and... well, explain. Instead, the treasure map dictates a ridiculous solution that demands a monstrous leap of faith. According to the map, when Indiana steps over the edge of that bottomless pit...a bridge will appear. Right! How about that bridge appears first and then Indiana traipses across it? Nope. That's not the plan.

Even though I have seen the movie several times, my stomach lurches when Indiana closes his eyes, takes a deep breath, and cautiously steps into absolutely nothing but air. If the treasure map is wrong, Indiana is dead. Fortunately, the map is correct, the bridge does appear, and Indiana Jones races across to safety, resuming his quest.

Gideon and Indiana Jones have a lot in common when it comes to faith. "Am I not sending you?" God asked Gideon, as if that fact explained it all. Actually, it does explain it all. God strengthens us *as we go*. When it comes to trusting God and the only thing that really matters is the fact that He sends us. Faith is a deliberate choice to

believe God and to walk through our fear, knowing we can trust Him every step of the way.

Let's Pray

Father, I am afraid to step out in faith. I want to trust You, but my faith is weak. I don't understand how You can love someone like me...and to think that You have a special plan for my life is hard to believe. Help my unbelief, Lord. In Jesus's name, amen.

A Tough Cookie Crumbles

Sharon Jaynes

Today's Truth

For it is by grace you have been saved, through faith—and this is not from yourselves, it is the gift of God. (Ephesians 2:8)

Friend to Friend

Allan was a tough cookie. He didn't drink every day, but when he did, he usually got drunk and terrorized his family. On many occasions his outbursts resulted in shattered furniture, a battered wife, and terrified children. But something happened in his home that began a domino effect of miracles. His fourteen-year-old daughter put her trust in Jesus Christ as Lord and Savior. God's presence infiltrated their home and began to tenderize Allan's tough heart.

When Allan first heard the gospel, he felt that he had done too many horrible things to be forgiven. He couldn't understand God's grace or believe that it was available to him. "I'll go to church with you," he said, "but I've done too many bad things to ever be a Christian. I could never be good enough. God would never forgive me."

"Oh, Daddy," his young daughter explained. "None of us could ever be good enough. If we could be good enough, Jesus would not have had to come and die on the cross for our sins. He gave His life for us because He knew we could never be good enough to earn eternal life. The Bible says that salvation is a gift. All we have to do is accept the gift, open the package, and God does all the rest."

"But I don't deserve it," Allan continued.

"No one deserves it, Daddy," the girl continued. "The only thing we *do* deserve is hell. Grace is getting a gift we don't deserve, and mercy is *not* getting the punishment we do deserve. God wants to give you both!"

But Allan couldn't accept God's grace. It seemed too easy.

His daughter continued to pray.

Six years after his daughter's commitment to Christ, Allan was on the verge of a nervous breakdown. A business deal had gone terribly wrong, and Allan was about to be sued and exposed for God only knew what in a court of law. He was at the end of his rope…just where God wanted him.

And at the precise time on God's kingdom calendar, a distraught Allan left home and drove hundreds of miles to Pennsylvania where his wife was at a meeting. When he couldn't find her, he drove to the first church he saw. The pastor wasn't there, so the church secretary drew him a map to where a pastor she knew was in the woods, physically building his church. With map in hand, Allan traveled on.

"What can I do for you?" the preacher asked as he saw Allan approach.

"I need help," Allan replied. "I need you to pray for me."

"Come right over here," the jeans-clad pastor with a hammer in his hand motioned. "Let's sit on this log, and you can tell me your story."

For the next few hours, Allan poured out his heart to this stranger and told him everything he had ever done. Then the preacher put his arm around Allan and said, "Now, Allan, let me tell you my story."

Allan finally understood God's grace on that hot July day in the woods of Pennsylvania, and he accepted Jesus as his Savior. Allan had met a man who was transparent about his own life. That preacher was not ashamed of the scars in his own life, and Allan saw the grace and forgiveness of Christ displayed in a life that mirrored his own. Allan later explained, "That man had done everything I had done. I knew that if Jesus could forgive him and he could be a preacher, then He could forgive me too."

Allan was my dad.

Is there someone you are praying for today? Perhaps you've been praying for many years. I want to encourage you: don't give up. Trust that God will answer your prayer in His perfect time and in His perfect way.

Let's Pray

Jesus, I stand in the gap and pray for my friends and family to come to know You as Savior and Lord. I eagerly wait in anticipation for each one to say yes to You, and I have faith that You will bring it to pass. In Jesus's name, amen.

Trusting God with Your Tomorrows

Gwen Smith

Today's Truth

The LORD said to him, "Who gave man his mouth? Who makes him deaf or mute? Who gives him sight or makes him blind? Is it not I, the LORD? Now go; I will help you speak and will teach you what to say." (Exodus 4:11–12, NIV 1984 edition)

Friend to Friend

On the far side of a desert, high upon the mountain of God, a voice called out to Moses from within a curious, fiery bush. He had been tending the sheep of his father-in-law's flock, minding his own business, going about his normal day-in-day-out tasks when God spoke to him from the flames. On the day that God called Moses to a fresh and fiery mission. A mission of deliverance.

Once a noble prince of Egypt with the world at his feet, Moses had become a lowly shepherd with dust on his sandals. His crown had been traded in for a staff. The palace days were far behind Moses now. He fled them because of what he had done. Glancing to his left and

his right to be sure that no one would see what he was about to do, Moses took a horrible situation into his own hands and killed a man. He had murdered an Egyptian and covered the body with sand.

Fear and shame bombarded his heart so he fled—away from his dream-filled, royal future to a desert place of humble hiding. The door to his yesterdays was closed. Moses had moved on to a new place. His past was his past and he had no intention of returning to it. His life was different now. Normal, not noble.

Then God interrupted Moses's new normal. He made it undeniably clear that His plans for Moses were different. Bigger. God's intentions were for freedom—the freedom of His people, the Israelites, who were captives, *slaves* to Egypt. God called Moses to face the pains of his past so that the Israelites could face a future of freedom. His plans of emancipation required that Moses obey Him, listen to His voice, follow His instructions, and trust Him.

Moses quivered and doubted. He made excuses about why he couldn't do it. He felt completely unfit and unqualified for such a task. It was risky. But God met Moses at his doubts. He called him to courage and went on to use Moses as an instrument of deliverance, truth, power, and freedom. Yes, Moses made mistakes along the way, but God was powerful in, through, and in spite of each one. Through it all, God led as only God can. He led with power. He led with purpose. He led with love. And through Moses, God led His people to a new place of promise and freedom.

On the far side of Charlotte, North Carolina, high upon a mountain in a retreat center, a voice called out to me from within a curious and fiery story. I had been tending to my husband and children, to the laundry and the dishes, writing songs and leading worship at women's events, minding my own business, and going about my normal day-in-day-out tasks on the day that God spoke to my heart

through the testimony of another woman. On the day that God called me to a fresh and fiery mission. A mission of deliverance.

Once a sold-out, dream-filled God-girl, I had become a grace-embracing yet *disqualified-for-anything-big-because-of-what-I-had-done* God-girl. My *use-me-in-a-big-way-Lord* prayers had been traded in for average *can't-have-a-dream-anymore* faith-living. My God-dream days were far behind me. I had fled them because of what I had done in my junior year of college. Glancing to my left and right to be sure that no one would know what I was about to do, I took a horrible situation—an unplanned pregnancy—into my own hands and killed a baby. I robbed life from my own child when I had an abortion, and I covered over the death of my precious child with sands of compartmentalization and reason.

Fear and shame bombarded my heart, so I fled—away from God, away from my dream-filled, royal future to a desert place of heart-hiding. After a season of brokenness, God brought me to a place of beauty, forgiveness, and healing. I was restored and redeemed by scandalous, merciful grace. The door to my yesterdays was closed. I moved on to a new place in Christ. My past was my past and I had no intentions of returning to it—or to the God-dreams that swelled my heart when I was a young, sold-out Jesus lover. My life was different now. Normal, not dream-worthy.

Then God interrupted my new normal. He made it undeniably clear that His plans for me were different. Bigger. God's intentions were for freedom—the freedom of His people, the women who were captives, *slaves* to their life-wounds. God called me to face the pains of my past so that my Girlfriends in God might face a future of freedom when they hear my testimony. His plans of emancipation required that I obey Him, listen to His voice, follow His instructions, and trust Him.

I quivered and doubted. I made excuses about why I couldn't do it. I felt completely unfit and unqualified for such a task. It was risky. But God met me at my doubts. He called me to courage and is using my broken-into-beautiful story as an instrument of deliverance, truth, power, and freedom. Yes, I make mistakes along the way, but God is powerful in, through, and in spite of each one. Through each surrendered day, God is leading as only He can. With power, with purpose, with love. And I pray right now that this story—my story—will bring you to a new place of promise and freedom through the grace of Jesus Christ.

What fresh and fiery mission is God calling you to trust Him with, friend? Let me encourage you to stop with the excuses. I'm living proof that God will free anyone from her shame and can use anyone for His purpose. Step up to the burning bush—into God's presence. Listen to His voice. Obey. Follow. Take courage. Trust Him with your past and with your tomorrows. Allow His grace and love to decide what your mission should look like.

> But I have raised you up for this very purpose, that I might
> show you my power and that my name might be proclaimed
> in all the earth. (Exodus 9:16)

Let's Pray

Dear God, with a trembling heart, I approach Your throne of grace today in reverence and humility, fully aware that You are holy and I am not. Speak, Lord. Show me the plans You have for me. Bind me to Your Word and to Your strength so I will have the courage to obey. May my brokenness be restored for the beauty of Your glory. Please help me to trust You with my today and my tomorrows. In Jesus's name I pray, amen.

The Love of God

Mary Southerland

Today's Truth

Jesus said, "Let the little children come to me, and do not hinder them, for the kingdom of heaven belongs to such as these." (Matthew 19:14)

Friend to Friend

I have personally discovered that it is downright frustrating and completely impossible to live the Christian life when you are not a Christian. I tried. For years, I desperately struggled to trust God with only head knowledge of who He is and wants to be in my life. When that trust settled into my heart and life, well, life became a different journey altogether.

I grew up in a Christian home, attending church every time the doors were open. I sang all the right songs, spoke all the right words, and did all the right things in front of all the right people. I fervently prayed that my works would validate my faith and desperately hoped that by following the rules, I would please the Ruler. It was not until middle school that the spiritual integrity of a dynamic youth pastor

made me hunger and thirst for something more. I wanted to know God and experience His unconditional love.

One Sunday, I sat in my usual spot, clutching the back of the pew in front of me while wrestling with God over the condition of my soul and my eternal security. After all, I was a very active church member, a soloist and pianist for our worship services, and I even directed a children's choir. How embarrassing to walk down that aisle, admitting to everyone that I'd been living a lie.

My mind argued that I knew all about God—and then the deeper truth of that argument hit me. Yes, I knew *about* Him, but I didn't *know* Him. That night, I met Jesus. My problems did not disappear, but much of my stress did as I began to trust God. I mean *really* trust Him.

Over the years, I have been taught by some incredible men and women of faith, but none more precious or more powerful than our grandchildren. One of the highlights of my day is when our thirteen-month-old grandson is getting ready for bed. It is not *his* favorite time of the day, but his mom has a routine that works well. She gives Justus a bath, during which he absolutely soaks every square inch of the bathroom. Danna then wraps him in a big, fluffy towel and brings him to everyone so that they can see the "clean baby" and give him a good night kiss. Next come lotion and pajamas, followed by "Bah," which means, "It's time to read a book." The light in his room is then dimmed, the musical fish sing and dance across the ceiling… and Justus settles down in his crib with Elmo in one hand and his blanket in the other, falling fast asleep within seconds. In a perfect world, that scenario would play out every night.

The world, however, is far from perfect. On nights when Justus does not feel well or needs a few extra hugs, Danna will ask me if I would like to rock him. I know. It is a rotten job, but somebody has

to do it. I scoop that precious little man into my arms, and as we begin to rock, I begin to sing. I have quite a repertoire of "Mimi" ballads, but when I start to sing "Jesus Loves Me," Justus always looks up at me with his big brown eyes and grows very still until the song is finished. I put him in his crib, and he usually does go right to sleep. However, last night, it was a different story.

Danna has been teaching Justus sign language, and one of his favorite words to sign is *more*. When I finished singing and started to get up out of the rocking chair, Justus stretched out his chubby little hands and signed, "More." Did I sit back down and sing some more? Do birds fly? Do fish swim?

With tears streaming down my face, I sang "Jesus Loves Me" until he was sound asleep. I sat in the rocker, just holding him, thinking about how very much I loved this baby boy. In that quiet moment, the Holy Spirit whispered to my heart, *"Mary, Jesus loves you, too."* As Justus and I rocked a few minutes longer, the stress of the day melted away, and I revisited the moment I met Jesus and first experienced His unchanging love. That quiet celebration filled my heart and left no room for anything but the love of God. Yes, Jesus loves me, and He loves you, too.

Oh, the love of God!

That's what trusting God is really all about. Jesus loves us so much that He gave His life so we could have abundant life here on earth and eternal life when we leave. Jesus loves you, this I know—and not just because the Bible tells me so, but because He shows you every single day.

You may find yourself in a frightening place filled with darkness and doubt. Your fragile heart may be wondering if God even knows where you are. He does. You think that because you cannot see the hand of God or sense His presence, it means He is not working.

Nothing could be further from the truth, girlfriend. We may not understand or even like His process, but God is *always* at work in our lives. He will always love you. Rest assured, God really is in control.

He will come through for you—and you can trust Him.

Let's Pray

Father, I come to You, thanking You for the love You have given me through the life and death of Your Son, Jesus Christ. Please help me to walk in that love every day with the faith of a child. In Jesus's name, amen.

Now It's Your Turn

TIME FOR REFLECTION

- Scripture is clear about the fact that we were created to need one another. A shared load is always a lighter load. Read 1 Thessalonians 5:14: "And we urge you, brothers and sisters, warn those who are idle and disruptive, encourage the disheartened, help the weak, be patient with everyone."

  Now think about the people in your life and answer the following questions:

  Who needs motivation (idle)?

  _____

  Who needs courage (disheartened)?

  _____

  Who needs strength (weak)?

  _____

  Who needs understanding (impatient)?

  _____

  Pray for each of these people and ask God to use you to encourage them.

- Read and memorize Hebrews 11:1: "Now faith is confidence in what we hope for and assurance about what we do not see." How

would you define *confidence* and *assurance* as it relates to your faith in God?

- Think about the following definition of *faith,* using an acronym: Forsaking All, I Trust Him. What does *all* mean in your life?

- Read what Jesus said in Matthew 17:20: "Truly I tell you, if you have faith as small as a mustard seed, you can say to this mountain, 'Move from here to there,' and it will move. Nothing will be impossible for you." What is the mountain in your life today? What one step can you take to move the mountain with faith instead of fear?

- Read 1 Thessalonians 5:11: "Therefore encourage one another and build each other up." Girlfriend, give somebody a high five! We *so* need to have this kind of friend and be this kind of friend. We need to be this kind of wife, mother, employee, sister, daughter, and neighbor. The kind that fills others with encouragement and builds them up. How can you apply this verse to the relationships in your life?

- Remember how Allan saw Jesus in that preacher in the woods of Pennsylvania? Just suppose the man had kept his past a secret and not told Allan his story. What do you think would have happened that day? Is God calling you to live a more transparent life?

- Read John 10:4 (NLT): "After he has gathered his own flock, he walks ahead of them, and they follow him because they know his voice."

    Think about the relationship between the sheep and the shepherd. The shepherd is always ahead of his sheep—out in front—which means that any attack on the sheep means first attacking the shepherd. What

peace and security we can have knowing that God goes before us through every valley and over every mountain of life. He knows what tomorrow holds and will give us everything we need to face it.

- Wrap up your response time with prayer. Move from confession, to adoration, to thanksgiving, and end with your petitions (personal prayer needs).

Your GiG Trust Adventure Journal

Spend a few moments contemplating and journaling about some of the scriptural truths that moved your heart as you read the devotions this week. Then write a prayer of response to God.

_____

_____

_____

_____

_____

_____

_____

_____

_____

_____

_____

_____

_____

_____

_____

_____

_____

_____

_____

_____

_____

_____

_____

_____

_____

_____

_____

_____

Therefore encourage one another and build each other up.
(1 Thessalonians 5:11)

ACKNOWLEDGMENTS

We would like to thank the many men and women who made this book possible:

Bill Jensen, our agent and guy-friend in God who cheers us on.

Our husbands—Steve, Brad, and Dan—who put up with our stacks of paper, late-night writing, and repeated requests of "Honey, can you read this and tell me what you think?"

Crosswalk.com, which debuted our Girlfriends in God devotions many years ago and continues to allow us to minister each weekday to women around the world.

BibleGateway.com, which has also locked arms with us in ministry to share the hope and healing of Jesus Christ.

All our Girlfriends in God who receive our daily devotions and keep asking the question "Where can I buy your GiG book?"

Our heavenly Father who equips us, our Savior Jesus who envelops us, and the precious Holy Spirit who empowers us.

TRUST-BUILDING SCRIPTURES

Be strong and courageous, do not be afraid or tremble at them, for the LORD your God is the one who goes with you. He will not fail you or forsake you. (Deuteronomy 31:6, NASB)

Those who know your name trust in you,
    for you, LORD, have never forsaken those who seek you.
        (Psalm 9:10)

But I trust in your unfailing love;
    my heart rejoices in your salvation.
I will sing the LORD's praise,
    for he has been good to me. (Psalm 13:5–6)

The LORD says, "I will guide you along the best pathway for
        your life.
    I will advise you and watch over you." (Psalm 32:8, NLT)

Commit your way to the LORD;
    trust in him and he will do this:
He will make your righteous reward shine like the dawn,
    your vindication like the noonday sun. (Psalm 37:5–6)

I waited patiently for the LORD;
    he turned to me and heard my cry.

He lifted me out of the slimy pit,
>out of the mud and mire;
he set my feet on a rock
>and gave me a firm place to stand. (Psalm 40:1–2)

Why am I discouraged?
>Why is my heart so sad?
I will put my hope in God!
>I will praise him again—
>my Savior and my God! (Psalm 42:5–6, NLT)

Then call on me when you are in trouble,
>and I will rescue you,
>and you will give me glory. (Psalm 50:15, NLT)

But I am like an olive tree
>flourishing in the house of God;
I trust in God's unfailing love
>for ever and ever. (Psalm 52:8)

When I am afraid, I put my trust in you.
In God, whose word I praise—
>in God I trust and am not afraid.
What can mere mortals do to me? (Psalm 56:3–4)

The LORD says, "I will rescue those who love me.
>I will protect those who trust in my name.
When they call on me, I will answer;
>I will be with them in trouble.
>I will rescue and honor them.

I will reward them with a long life
 and give them my salvation." (Psalm 91:14–16, NLT)

I praise your name for your unfailing love and faithfulness;
for your promises are backed
 by all the honor of your name. (Psalm 138:2, NLT)

Trust in the LORD with all your heart
 and lean not on your own understanding;
in all your ways submit to him,
 and he will make your paths straight. (Proverbs 3:5–6)

She is clothed with strength and dignity;
she can laugh at the days to come. (Proverbs 31:25)

Surely God is my salvation;
 I will trust and not be afraid.
The LORD, the LORD himself, is my strength and my defense;
 he has become my salvation. (Isaiah 12:2)

You will keep in perfect peace
 those whose minds are steadfast,
 because they trust in you. (Isaiah 26:3)

But those who hope in the LORD
 will renew their strength.
They will soar on wings like eagles;
 they will run and not grow weary,
 they will walk and not be faint. (Isaiah 40:31)

You whom I took from the ends of the earth,
    and called from its farthest corners,
saying to you, "You are my servant,
    I have chosen you and not cast you off";
fear not, for I am with you;
    be not dismayed, for I am your God;
I will strengthen you, I will help you,
    I will uphold you with my righteous right hand.
        (Isaiah 41:9–10, ESV)

When you pass through the waters,
    I will be with you;
and when you pass through the rivers,
    they will not sweep over you.
When you walk through the fire,
    you will not be burned;
    the flames will not set you ablaze. (Isaiah 43:2)

Let the one who walks in the dark,
    who has no light,
trust in the name of the LORD
    and rely on their God. (Isaiah 50:10)

"For I know the plans I have for you," declares the LORD,
"plans to prosper you and not to harm you, plans to give you
hope and a future." (Jeremiah 29:11)

Do not let your hearts be troubled. You believe in God;
believe also in me."(John 14:1)

I am leaving you with a gift—peace of mind and heart. And the peace I give is a gift the world cannot give. (John 14:27, NLT)

And I am convinced that nothing can ever separate us from his love. Death can't, and life can't. The angels can't, and the demons can't. Our fears for today, our worries about tomorrow, and even the powers of hell can't keep God's love away. Whether we are high above the sky or in the deepest ocean, nothing in all creation will ever be able to separate us from the love of God that is revealed in Christ Jesus our Lord. (Romans 8:38–39, NLT 1996 edition)

Do not worry about anything. But pray and ask God for everything you need. And when you pray, always give thanks. And God's peace will keep your hearts and minds in Christ Jesus. The peace that God gives is so great that we cannot understand it (Philippians 4:6–7, ICB)

I have learned the secret of being content in any and every situation, whether well fed or hungry, whether living in plenty or in want. I can do all this through him who gives me strength. (Philippians 4:12–13)

And my God will meet all your needs according to the riches of his glory in Christ Jesus. (Philippians 4:19)

For God has not given us a spirit of fear, but of power and of love and of a sound mind. (2 Timothy 1:7, NKJV)

ABOUT *Girlfriends* IN GOD

GIRLFRIENDS IN GOD is a nondenominational devotional and conference ministry that crosses generational and racial boundaries to bring the body of Christ together as believers. Just as God sent Ruth to Naomi and Mary to Elizabeth, God continues to use women to encourage and equip other women in their spiritual journeys.

Through daily online devotions, conferences, published books, CDs, and music videos, God is using this incredible team of women to bring the hope and healing of Jesus Christ to a hurting world.

GIRLFRIENDS IN GOD conferences are "turnkey" events designed to meet the needs of any ministry, church, or organization desiring to impact the lives of women for Christ. The GiG team helps women experience the height, width, and depth of God's love in a world cloaked in hopelessness and despair. The leadership team of Girlfriends in God is committed to helping women grow deeper in their relationships with God and soar higher in freedom and faith.

God is using this incredible team of Girlfriends in God to bring the hope and healing of Jesus Christ to a hurting world. The team includes Sharon Jaynes, Gwen Smith, and Mary Southerland.

SHARON JAYNES is an international conference speaker whose in-depth knowledge of Scripture, combined with an engaging storytelling style, keeps listeners on the edge of their seats. Peppered with laughter and salted with tears, Sharon shares from her heart how to find peace and purpose in the pain of your past. Her passion is to encourage, equip, and empower women to walk in confidence as

they grasp their true identity as a child of God and co-heir with Christ. She's the author of seventeen books and multiple Bible studies and is a popular guest on radio and television programs. To learn more, see www.sharonjaynes.com.

GWEN SMITH is a speaker, author, songwriter, and worship leader who inspires women toward the heart of God through stories, songs, and Scripture. Her fun, enthusiastic, and relatable communication style puts audiences at ease and bridges generational, denominational, and racial divides. Gwen has helped thousands of women experience how the Word of God and the power of grace, through Jesus Christ, rejuvenates faith and enriches lives. She is the author of *Broken into Beautiful* and has recorded six CD projects of God-centered adoration that encourage listeners to move beyond their current level of intimacy with Him. To learn more visit www.gwensmith.net.

MARY SOUTHERLAND is "the Stress Buster," a leader at helping women manage stress and find joy in their daily lives. Mary is an internationally popular speaker at women's retreats and conferences as well as events for women in ministry. With transparency and humor, Mary wraps God's message of hope and love around the tough issues of life, inspiring women to step out in radical obedience to God. Mary's experience as a pastor's wife and the Women's Ministry Motivator has helped leaders across the world embrace ministry challenges and develop essential leadership skills. Mary has written four books that lead women to discover who they are in Christ and how to live the life of victory for which they were created. To learn more, visit www.marysoutherland.com

These three women have joined together to bring you inspirational devotions and conferences that will change your life. No matter where you are on your journey toward the heart of God, Girlfriends in God will help you take the next step closer.

To learn more about Girlfriends in God, to sign up for their free daily e-devotions, or to inquire about hosting a Girlfriends in God conference, visit www.GirlfriendsInGod.com or write to:

Girlfriends in God
PO Box 725
Matthews, NC 28106

And remember, visit www.GirlfriendsInGod.com
to share your trusting-God story.